# Trajectory

www.trajectoryjournal.com

*Chris Helvey* **Editor/Publisher**
*Gina Helvey* **Associate Editor**
*Clay Gibson* **Associate Editor**
*Myra Summers* **Layout/Design**

Issue 20, Spring 2020 © Helvey Enterprises 2020. Trajectory (ISSN 2158-1231). Periodicals Postage Paid at Frankfort, KY. Published semi-annually by Helvey Enterprises, PO Box 655, Frankfort, KY 40602-0655. Phone: 502-330-4746. Email: adobechris@hotmail.com ISBN 978-7337936-2-9. Subscription rates: 1 year (2 issues) $20.00; 2 years (4 issues) $35.00. Single copy price $12.00.

Back Issues: Request in writing to *Trajectory*, PO Box 655, Frankfort, KY 40602-0655, or visit www.trajectoryjournal.com

**Submissions:** *Trajectory* accepts submissions throughout the year. We are interested only in original poetry, fiction, creative non-fiction, memoirs, book reviews, author interviews, and black & white photos and art. Submit via USPS only (no electronic submissions accepted). Submit 3-5 poems, short stories up to 10,000 words, and copies only of black & white photos/art. While we will consider all work, we generally are not interested in fiction/poetry for children, YA manuscripts, fantasy, romance, sci-fi, or horror submissions. Always include a brief bio (75 words or less). Submissions sent without an SASE will not receive a response. Submit to above address.

Cover Photo by Morgan Smith: The two Mixteca Indian boys on the cover migrated up to Juárez with their families from the very poor state of Oaxaca in search of a better life. They're trying to survive with their music.

# FROM THE FAR SIDE OF THE DESK

## *Happy Birthday Trajectory!*

I **KNOW IT'S HARD TO BELIEVE,** but with this issue (Issue 20) *Trajectory* will be 10 years old (two issues per year – you do the math...). When I launched *Trajectory* all those many years ago, I never dreamed we would print twenty issues. And I mean **we**. For without your wonderful stories, poems, photos, memoirs, etc., your financial support (my special thanks to all who have subscribed, who bought an extra copy [or two, or three, or...], or who simply sent me a few dollars) and especially your encouraging emails, letters, phone calls, and your friendship this special journal of ours never would have survived.

I would also be terribly remiss if I did not thank three very special people whose behind the scenes efforts have made each and every issue possible.

First, my wonderful wife and Assistant Editor, Gina Helvey. Not only has she put up with long hours (and we won't mention my rantings and ravings), but she has caught more misplaced commas, dangling participles, and hanging gerunds than any one person should be forced to face. Plus, she has been a huge financial help since the first day we began.

Next, Myra Summers, who has been the layout/format/publishing maestro for every issue. She is the one who, each issue, takes that glorious mishmash of poems, stories, memoirs, and assembles them into a coherent order. She lays out the Table of Contents, formats the Author Bios, and makes every one of the dozens of edits I note required for each issue. In addition, she has put up with me, and the drafts, and edits, and more edits of my own writings for more years than either one of us probably wants to admit (which surely automatically qualifies her for sainthood).

Finally, Clay Gibson, the man solely responsible for setting up, updating, and maintaining the *Trajectory* website (www.trajectoryjournal.com). Without his efforts and dedication dozens of original stories, poems, and photos might never have been shared with the world. In addition, he has contributed many of the photos you have seen over the years, and he has produced covers for at least two of my books.

So, when the planets align for you, please send a few well-earned thanks and blessings winging toward the wonderful trio noted above.

Now for the other side of the coin…

I won't get maudlin or melodramatic about this. Instead, I'll just pretend I'm Jack Webb in *Dragnet* and give you the facts, just the facts.

Despite the wonderful support from many of you, the bottom line is *Trajectory* loses money with every issue. We have had some wonderfully faithful subscribers and many folks have ordered the extra copy, or copies, from time to time. However, the reality is that *Trajectory* goes in the red to the tune of a few hundred dollars each issue.

Now, going in I never expected to make my fortune with a literary journal and I don't mind subsidizing this publication to some degree. However, being an old retired varmint, my resources are not unlimited and so I thought I'd let you know that unless *Trajectory* experiences a significant financial turnaround over the next few months I can't guarantee publication beyond Issue 21 (Fall 2020).

Please know I remain optimistic. We have launched a subscription push and are off to a good start. In addition, we have finally bowed to reality and begun to charge shipping costs for extra copy orders. We've kept this as low as we could – only $3 per order. Now that's not $3 per book; it's $3 total per order, regardless of whether an individual orders one book, or four, or ten. As I noted earlier, I'm not in the literary journal game to make money – I just have a limit on how much I can afford to subsidize.

I'm also buying lottery tickets, hoping for a large income tax return, and (with apologies to Ray Stevens) desperately searching for that extremely valuable 8x10 glossy of Bo Diddley suitable for framing.

If you've been thinking about taking out a subscription to *Trajectory* or buying a few extra copies of this issue (or even a copy of a back issue), now would be a good time to act. All contributions will be gratefully accepted and much appreciated.

Okay, enough already with the gloom and doom. Let's turn our attention to more pleasant matters.

**Trajectory Alumni:**

**Ruth Holzer:** Ruth has a wonderful chapbook, *Why We're Here*, out from Presa Press (www.presapress.com). By the way, Ruth is a seven-time Pushcart nominee!

**t. kilgore splake:** t., who has had so many wonderful books/chapbooks of his unique haiku-like poems published, has a brand new one out – and it's one of his best. Check out *Winter Whispers* from Cyberwit.net. Not only does *Winter Whispers* contain some wonderful new poems from the Bard of Michigan, but some of his finest photos as well, and they're in color!! As you may recall, over the issues t. has contributed many fine photos to this publication.

**ayaz daryl nielsen:** A frequent *Trajectory* contributor, daryl's latest is *kissing the stitches* from Scars Publications (http://scars.tv). Here's a sneak preview "scent of honeysuckle/through an open window/mother's last breath." Those lines hit me like a brutal solar plexus blow from Ali in his prime! I guarantee there's a novel lurking in those ten words.

**Alan Catlin:** Alan Catlin has recently published three new books of poetry (talk about being on a roll!!): *Asylum Garden after Van Gogh* from Dos Madres, *Lessons in Darkness* from Luchador Press, and *The Idea of North* from Cyberwit. He is the editor of *Misfit Magazine* online and a long-time *Trajectory* fave – poems and stories. I've already purchased my copy of *Lessons in Darkness* and am, as always, impressed by Alan's ability to tell a powerful, often dark, story in just a few poetic lines. So far "Jesus' Son" is my favorite. By the way another of the poems in this volume, "Dead Calm," was originally published in *Trajectory.*

**New Venture:**

I am in the process of launching a new, hybrid writing project where I will undertake a joint venture with another author who wants to publish a book, but doesn't want to go down the mainstream publishing path to do so. Basic concept is we share the costs and the royalties, while I provide the book layout, cover design, and editorial services. Plus, I handle all the print on demand details with Kindle Direct Press. My vision to produce both a paperback and an e-book, with pricing for both to be determined by mutual agreement. Publication will be under the Trajectory Journal imprint.

I've already begun the first of these joint efforts (each of us has written a novella and will combine those – a duet of novellas if you will), and have another book in the wings. If you have questions or would like more details, reach out to me at adobechris@hotmail.com or 502-330-4746.

**By the way,** I'm still looking for a couple of

readers. That is folks who will read my work and then give me back honest feedback – good and bad. In turn, I'll do the same for you. You can contact me anytime at adobechris@hotmail.com or 502-330-4746.

**Now, on to Issue 20!!**

What a great lineup we have for you – lots of those writers and poets whose work you've enjoyed over the years (folks like J.S. Kierland, Brian James Lewis, Cathy Porter, Ted Jonathan, and Vincent Tomeo to name a few), plus some exciting new talents whose work I really believe you'll enjoy reading (like Marion Byers, Tamara Wilson, Steve Flairty, and Blair Ewing. Plus we've got another thought-provoking photo essay from Morgan Smith, brand new flash fiction from Anthony Herles (who I think writes flash fiction as well as anybody), and even the first chapter of my latest novel, *Yard Man*. Please enjoy!

*Chris*

P.S. My next novel, *Dancing on the Rim*, is scheduled for release by Wings ePress on April 1, 2020. Both an e-book and paperback edition will be available from Amazon.

# In Order of Appearance

# Tamra Wilson

## Church Camp

ON MONDAY MORNING MAMA, who had been draggy since Daddy walked out, was in such a cheery mood you would have thought she'd had a fresh haircut. She drank her second cup of coffee, then pulled her "cold cash" from the freezer, the place she hid spare money to avoid the temptation to spend it.

She counted a thin wad of small bills. "We're taking a little trip."

"Where?" I said.

"It's a surprise," she said.

My stomach tightened. I didn't trust her surprises with all the mayhem we'd been through that summer – Daddy leaving, Mama moving us to a run-down apartment and Billy gone to camp. Mama wasn't packing a suitcase, so this couldn't be an overnight trip.

"Dirk said we can drop in on the camp whenever we want and it so happens I would want to do that today."

"It isn't time for Billy to come home," I said. I knew exactly when he was coming: August 11, 1962, five whole days away.

"We're going to pay him a visit. Get dressed." She opened the wardrobe.

"Does he know?"

"No, I told you it's a surprise," she said.

Anyone taking car attendance here would know ours was never gone long, certainly not for a whole day at a time.

We filled up at the Deep Rock station because they gave Green Stamps. Mama lifted her sunglasses and primped in the rear-view mirror, adding more lipstick. She looked pretty in her bright blue sheath which had been her shopping outfit back in Tampa. She fluffed the hem to cool her legs. The car already smelled of midday heat.

The gas man sprayed blue liquid on the windshield, then took a rubber blade on a stick and wiped each stroke from top to bottom, carefully lifting the wipers. I thought he was an even-enough fellow until he winked back at Mama and she grinned. I felt my neck grow pink. Why Mama had to flirt with every man alive was beyond me.

"Ma'am, I see your plate's from Florida," he said.

"That's right." She removed her sunglasses.

"Whereabouts?"

"Tampa," she said.

"Bet it's a hot one down there today."

"No doubt." She handed him a few crumpled bills from her change purse. Mama's surprise had already cost $3.10 and we hadn't left town.

He flipped coins from a little metal box on his belt. "I know a couple of fellers in the Air Force down there."

Mama didn't act like this rang any bells. She counted her change. "How about my stamps?"

He fished into his shirt pocket and counted out a strip of them with grime-stained fingers. Mama flashed him a grateful smile, the kind she'd used before we moved away from home.

She leaned up to inspect the windshield. "We're squeaky clean now," she said as she started the engine.

But I didn't feel clean at all. My backside was still oozy. I'd put on the only dress left that didn't have stains down the front, but it smelled musty from hanging in the wardrobe.

I opened the glove box to find the Green Stamps savings book to stick the stamps on the pages. "Whoa! Did you see how nasty his hands were? There's no telling what you can pick up. You use a sponge when we get home."

I slipped the loose stamps into the book and closed the glove box. Here she was worried about health when she was drinking Nervine lady's tonic as if there was no tomorrow.

This was our first trip out of town since we'd moved to Wakefield, and it was some kind of fun to see something new. Rows of soybeans rushed by like tufts of chenille on a green bedspread. Mama clicked on the radio and flipped the dial muttering about no news stations. She finally settled for a song we'd heard all summer: Gene Pitney's "The Man Who Shot Liberty Valance."

"What's a valance?" I asked.

She motioned her hand across the top of the steering wheel. "It's the short curtain at the top of a window."

I remembered that Grandma June had one in her kitchen with little drawings of egg beaters and spatulas and spice jars. "Why did they name him after a curtain?"

She shrugged. "It's just a name." She pushed the lighter knob on the dashboard. "How about grabbing me a cigarette?"

I fished around in her pocketbook.

"Your last name is your family's," she said. "Your folks give you your first name."

I already knew all that. I hadn't passed second grade for nothing. I'd asked about Putnam once and Daddy had laughed and said we got our last name because our people in the olden days liked "puttin' em" in their place. Names meant something extra to Mama.

"Why would they name a boy Liberty?"

She poked the lighter back into the dashboard. "I don't know. Maybe she likes the Statue of Liberty."

I knew Miss Liberty from my silver dollar. She had the curliest hair in the world bar none. Mama had given me a couple of home permanents back before she gave up on making me look cute. That's when she gave me a boyish pixie cut and declared jeweled barrettes and hair clips a waste. I'd never have pretty hair to tie in ribbons or plait in fancy braids like girls at my school. I cried when Mama wasn't looking.

The radio played commercials about farm chemicals and crop hail insurance. Life here was all about growing things and making sure you did a good job of it. You planted a field, it had to grow. Your life depended on it. Anything uninvited must be removed, like weeds in Grandma June's flower beds.

"Won't Billy be surprised." Mama smiled to herself. "He wrote to June that the Schoonovers have already been up to see Mike."

Of course she wouldn't want to be outdone by them, never mind the fact that this trip would shrink precious money, something that I wasn't about to point out. Mama was going to do what Mama wanted. She'd escape Wakefield for a while. At the top of the hour she turned up the radio to catch the news.

*Investigation continues into the death of actress Marilyn Monroe, found early Sunday from an apparent suicide.*

She looked over at me. "My God, did you hear that?" She turned the newscast to full volume. "Miss Monroe, age 36, was found dead in bed yesterday of what appears to be an overdose of sleeping pills.... Fans around the world are deeply shocked by the star's premature and tragic death."

Mama slowed the car. Her hands were shaking on the steering wheel when she pulled over. She searched for a hanky as we sat idling in a farmer's driveway. I didn't know what I'd do if she took one of her sick spells. She had long admired Marilyn Monroe though she didn't consider her a saved Christian, what with her wild living and naked-book poses. I imagined the beautiful star in a white flowing robe knocking on Heaven's door like a picture of Jesus in Billy's Bible, only it would be doubtful that the door would ever open.

"See if there's one of my tonics in the glove box," Mama said, gasping.

I plucked the bottle from a nest of road maps. She took a quick sip, then dabbed away tears. "Why oh Lord do the beautiful die young?"

It was noon before we reached Camp Nazareth. The place was the biggest clump of trees for miles around, and the parking lot looked all but deserted.

She wasted no time breezing into the camp office, demanding to see Billy Graham. The lady at the desk gave her an odd look until she explained that it was her son's given name. The woman broke into a broad smile as if she understood a joke.

It was lunch time and children in white camp t-shirts were eating fried chicken under a clump of shade trees. Billy ran over and gave Mama a hug while she stood stiff as a board, unable to hug him back.

I stared at the chicken leg on his paper plate. "Got anything for us?"

He made a face. "You want to *eat* here?"

Mama set her handbag down. "We haven't driven eighty miles to starve to death."

She sent me over to the window where they handed out the food. When I returned, she had joined Billy and Mike Schoonover, Billy's friend from our church, at the table. She asked us to bow our heads. The next thing out of her mouth was, "Isn't it terrible news about Marilyn Monroe?"

Of course she had to explain what she was talking about, and it was all she could do to keep her voice even. I hoped she wouldn't start crying like she'd done in the car. After she had heard that newscast, it had taken her several minutes to get back on the road, and then she had practically twisted the tuning knob off the radio for more updates.

Billy sat quietly. Mike wanted news from home: how his little league team was doing, (I had no idea), whether the church was going to have a hayride for the kids (I hadn't heard of it) and if the Rexall had any new Duncan yoyos (as if this was something I would check on).

He concluded, "You don't know much, do you Squirt?"

I squinted back at him as I kept eating. The chicken was cold and dry, but I was so hungry that I was half-finished eating before I remembered to tell Billy that Daddy showed up last week from wherever it was he'd run off to.

Mama looked embarrassed, then proceeded with, "He says he'll be back before long so we can decide about the house."

Billy smiled. "Did you hear that, Mike? We're getting a new house."

I was stunned. Daddy had said nothing about a house. All he did was pack up and leave. It was as if she believed her own lies.

"When do we move?" Billy asked.

"We'll see."

"But Daddy said – "

Mama cut me off. "We can't live in that apartment forever. It's not healthy."

Healthy? The way she smoked cigarettes and kept the blinds pulled, she had me fooled. I looked down at my pale skinny legs. During an ordinary summer, I'd turn freckled as a ripe banana. This year I hadn't been outdoors long enough to grow sunburn lines. But maybe she and Daddy were playing a game, cooking up a secret plot to surprise us with a new house. As gullible as I was at the time, I wanted to believe her.

"Are we going to stay in Wakefield?" Billy asked.

"We'll see." Her eyes drifted off to nowhere in particular.

Billy seemed bored by all the talk about our house. As soon as he could get a word in, he told us about the Bible play he was in.

"What part are you, Mike?" I asked, relieved for the distraction.

"I'm Bartholomew. He was one of the disciples."

Since that character never said a word in the New Testament, Mike would do just fine.

"Did they cut your head off yet?" I asked Billy.

"Nope," he touched his neck. "They don't do that until the last night of camp."

He told us how he had to kneel in front of a stump that was placed behind a backlit sheet. The audience would see the ax drop. Then the executioner would hold up a fake head.

"You don't really see his head come off." Mike said.

"You don't?" I sounded disappointed.

Everyone looked at me, amused, when Mike offered, "They go out to the cemetery and dig up this old dead guy and – "

"He's pulling your leg," Mama said.

"It's really a coconut wearing a Halloween wig," Billy explained.

Mike excused himself to run off with another boy. It was a white-hot day – too warm to stand on a ball diamond waiting for something to happen. Knowing what a sorry player Billy was, he'd be sent to the outfield to chew clover petals.

We were all three watching the game form up. I got a little worried that, with Billy gone, Mama might start up with the house business again. If she did, it wasn't going to end well. "Guess what?" I said, calculating the better distraction. "Daddy had a baby sister."

Billy rolled his eyes. "What's the punch line?"

"No, he really did. Grandma June said so. Her name was Dorothy and they called her Dot. Only she died a long time ago."

"How come we never heard about her?" Mama said. She blew a halo of smoke over our heads as a softball game squared off.

The three of us watched. "Can I go home now?" Billy said. "I'm about ready."

"You still have a whole week left, Billy."

"But I hate it here. It's all buggy and Mike isn't my best friend up here like I thought he'd be. Everyone makes fun of my name when they do roll call. I'm Billy Graham, the Old Crusader. And they put sand in my sheets. One boy even peed on my pillow."

I was surprised my big brother the know-it-all was being so honest. He may have to sleep on a pee-pot pillow, but what did he think he'd be coming home to? Did he even get my letter? *Mama beet me last night. Come home quick so I won't get kilt. Please hurry! If you can't come right away, pray hard.*

"Please Mama. I don't like it here," he begged.

She flicked ashes over the edge of the picnic table. "You have a camp counselor, don't you? Why don't you talk to him?"

"I have. He tells me to be a good sport. I hate sports. All they do is make us play softball or horseshoes. It's worse than school."

"Stop whining. You got to come up here. It's a far sight more than I ever got to do at your age," she said.

He rolled his eyes from Mama to me, but I knew better than to show him any emotion. If I started to boohoo we'd both turn to warm butter.

"I want to go home, Mama."

She held her jaw as if she had a toothache. "I don't raise quitters, young man. You're going to have to tough it out."

"But it's too hard."

"Don't tell me what's hard. I had to stretch my dimes to get you ready to come up here. You wanted to come, you make the best of it. What will Mike do if you leave? What would the people at church say if you quit? Brother Dirk worked hard to make this possible for you."

Everything was about what other people thought:

18

church people, the camp people, and now Brother Dirk, our preacher, who found Billy a "campership" so he could afford to go. The truth was, the only ones who would know or care about the campership were Grandma June, who I figured paid for it, and Brother Dirk who did the begging for it. Mike wouldn't care if Billy left. Obviously he had other friends. Still, I couldn't believe that Mama didn't cave. Billy was her forever favorite, but right now she wasn't showing him an ounce of sympathy.

We all looked up when man in a camp shirt cleared his throat. "Sorry ma'am, but we don't allow smoking here."

She paused. "Excuse me?"

"I'm Rob David, the director," he said open-ended, as if he'd asked himself a question. "As a Christian camp, we grownups must set a good example."

Mama frowned. "Good example?"

"It's for the children's sake. We teach clean living here."

She snubbed the half-smoked cigarette out on the picnic table. It smoldered in the chipped paint, growing a dark wound. "There. Hope that makes you happy."

I thought he would blast her for making burn marks on the table. Instead, he said, "Ma'am, I appreciate your understanding."

"Oh I do *understand.*" Her voice was as thick as when she yelled at Daddy. She rose from the bench. "What else do you do, Mr. David, shoot your visitors with slingshots? How about hospitality, do you teach that? That's part of being a good Christian, isn't it?"

It was clear he wasn't going to answer. "This is your son?" he said.

"Yes. This is *Billy Graham* Putnam."

I cringed for Billy. No one could top the churchy name she'd given him, and here she was, reciting the whole shebang.

Mr. David twitched the corner of his mouth. "I

don't want to be unpleasant, Mrs. Putnam."

"Oh I'm sure you don't. You want to set a good example." I could tell she'd had fire-brand religion on her mind for a long time.

Billy and I sat there stunned as she lit into the man like an evangelist, quoting scripture about "going to Hell" and resembling "one of the Four Horsemen of the Apocalypse," thumping the picnic table as if it were a pulpit. He wasn't Daddy, but he was a man, and, so far, few of them had given her much to feel good about.

After Mr. David slinked away, Mama declared herself more than ready to leave. Billy got a nervous look on his face, and then he bit his lip as if he was trying to think something up quick, considering and rejecting ideas as soon as they came. Finally, he settled on his last stall tactic. "Let me show you my cabin." Reluctantly, she let him lead us to a grove of buckeye trees. But she said it had better be quick. We had eighty miles ahead of us, and he had his own camp obligations. The cabin resembled a tool shed, slightly less open-air than a corn crib, with bunk beds on each side of the narrow room.

I pointed to a dark spot on the rug beside his bed. "Is this where Mabel set the table?"

"Yes," he said, telling Mama, "She means where that kid threw up."

"Charming." Mama stood, arms folded, drumming her fingers on her elbows.

He led us to an indoor chapel with a concrete floor. A wooden platform had been built up front with a white curtain stretched across a clothesline.

"They shine a light from behind, so we're shadow figures."

"Do you get to make animal shapes?" I asked.

"This isn't Noah's ark," Mama snapped.

"You will come see the play, won't you?" Billy asked.

She swayed from one foot to the other. "I don't

know. It's a long ways up here."

I couldn't believe she'd hesitate to see Billy perform. Most days we didn't have anything better to do but listen for trains and count floor tiles.

"We can come, can't we, Mama?"

She sighed. "I don't think so, Kelly. *Smokers* aren't welcome." A fresh cloud of disappointment came over Billy. His face turned blotchy, but he wouldn't let himself cry.

By the time we reached the parking lot, he sounded desperate. "Please can't I go home? It won't take me long to pack."

"Young man, the Lord allowed you to come up here. Do you think he'd want you to spit in His eye by running away?"

"No ma'am," he mumbled.

The argument was over.

Mama strutted ahead of us as I grabbed his sleeve. "Be glad you aren't home," I whispered.

"Why?"

I sliced a finger across my neck.

When we got to the car, I wondered if he might try to stow away in the back seat, but all he did was stand in the driveway like a lone post, shivering.

She started the motor. "Remember Jesus was tempted for forty days in the wilderness. The least you can do is endure another five."

Billy studied the ground as if she had said he belonged to another family. I waved goodbye, but I didn't let myself look at my brother directly for fear I'd cry for sure. As we pulled onto the highway, I couldn't help but feel sorry for him. Thanks to Mama and her hot-headed sermon, Billy would have to suffer payback from the camp director. Billy would say he was too old to cry though Mama had pushed him to it.

# Marion S. Byers

## Grandmother

Lived the poorest poor.
Scrubbed floors for a dollar a day.
Feeding three children is hard.

When your husband is hard.
When your husband
Loves a bottle,
More than he loves you.

Your mind was rich with memory
Of a young girl
Who would rather dance than eat.
Your mind alive with music, beaus
and dancing feet.

In your kitchen
You would laugh for joy
And think about it.

I surprised you at your door:
"Why, Marion, I'm so glad to see you."

Your laughter filled your house with joy,
We would drink tea, because I liked it.

But I listened to the girl
Who would rather dance than eat.

# *Signs*

Warning:
No life guard on duty.
Swim at your own risk.

I did even though I can't swim.
I swam anyway
Even though I don't know how.

I'm not afraid of swimming:
It's living at my own risk
That frightens me.


# *Because, being late,*

We walked home
Along the old road.
But I left,
And walked another way,
Through wide, new turned fields.
We met again
On the other side,
I had seen
An apple tree in bloom
And a nest of baby rabbits
While crossing

# Steve Flairty

# Irma Gall and Peggy Kemner

(An excerpt from *Kentucky's Everyday Heroes:
Ordinary People Doing Extraordinary Things,*
by Steve Flairty)

IRMA GALL, AMAZINGLY SPRY to be in her mid-eighties, was only too happy to show me her cabin, one she built on a wide space on the road at the base of a steep hillside just a few hundred yards from Stinking Creek.

"I'm a rock mason, and I believe in good foundations," she noted, pointing out the intricate meshing of native stones holding together a hewn-log frame house, wood set firmly on both vertical and horizontal planes. All told, Irma has lain over 500 tons of rocks in foundations, walls and fireplaces.

It comes naturally that she uses the word "foundations" in describing the cabin. Irma and her long-time friend, Peggy Kemner, dreamed of establishing good foundations, literally and metaphorically, when they decided over a half century ago to join their talents to, in their words, "lend a hand" to the poor and often uneducated people around Stinking Creek, in Knox County. They started their long tenure perceived as outsiders. No more is that true with the area locals today.

Since 1958 until recent years, as Peggy's health declined, the two have personified the concept of caring; they might be considered doing so in a westernized

Mother Teresa way. If Mother Teresa still lived, she might even learn a few things from them.

And what sustained acts of caring have Irma and Peggy brought to bear at Stinking Creek? When they met in the late fifties in Leslie County while doing mission work, Irma from Indiana and Peggy from Pennsylvania, they soon decided that their individual backgrounds could be put to use on a synergetic course. "I'll teach school and you deliver babies," recalled Irma. "We came over the mountain to Stinking Creek." And when they arrived in the poverty-stricken community, they did those things and much more.

But first, they had to find a place to live. How they got one showcases the remarkable character of the two women. A place to live came to be after initial resistance by the Stinking Creek folk, who were simply suspicious of their motives. But on a hot and dusty day in August 1958, the somewhat discouraged lookers came upon an old and weathered, framed two-story house. It sat pitifully amongst high horseweeds in bottom lands near a Stinking Creek tributary, Patterson Branch. Intrigued, Irma and Peggy walked down into the low land for a closer look. About all one could say of a positive nature was that the house was still standing; it would take imagination to see it as a livable home for humans.

"The flood of '57 had ravaged that house," explained Irma. "There were snake trails all through the house and dead birds. Some of the windows were gone and (also) part of the roof. But it was a six-room house, four rooms on the bottom and two on the top. We immediately thought: 'This is it. This is it!'"

They soon found the person who owned the property and bargained to allow them to move in. He was dubious about their request, but agreed to allow them to live there rent-free if they agreed to fix it up using their own labor and resources. They eagerly took the challenge and in what must have seemed an insurmountable task for most, they embraced the challenge and didn't look back.

"Doing the windows on the second floor, we put a long board sticking out and Peggy sat on it inside and I sat on it outside and put the panes in," explained Irma. There was mud to clean out, leaks to fix, and critters to fend off, and there would always be a threat of a flood from Patterson Branch. But the two women, tough and buoyed by their religious faith and tenacious spirit, rebuilt themselves a house that became a home.

In time, they acquired the property and hundreds of acres. The land became the base of operations for the organization known as Lend-a-Hand, where eventually a legion of humble souls saw their lives get better.

In those early days of their startup, Irma rode her horse over rough and hilly terrain to teach at Alex School in a one-room building some eight miles away. Peggy, a graduate of the acclaimed Frontier Nursing Service, also rode on horseback, but mostly drove a little red Jeep to serve as a midwife and attend to medical needs for the poor in their homes. When time was available, Irma traveled and assisted Peggy.

"Peggy delivered the first baby within three months there. Word got out quickly," remembered Irma. The two "do-gooders," as those mission-minded in Appalachia were often termed, believed that self-respect developed when receivers of help also took some personal responsibility whenever possible. Consequently, Peggy charged $25 for delivering the babies. Included in the service was both pre and post-natal care. Some paid with food (beans and rice was popular with Irma and Peggy), chickens, pigs and goats; that arrangement was just fine for the two of them.

She delivered more than 500 babies, some in log cabins, others in two or three-room houses and under and almost every situation imaginable. Peggy had no problem getting clients, and she quickly gained respect for her demonstrated expertise.

Besides teaching, Irma used her agrarian childhood

experiences to launch herself excitedly into farming on their bottom land, producing food for the two and also to share in the community. She acquired a tractor and other implements, such as a corn planter and plow, and built a barn and other outbuildings, and with that, raised an assortment of livestock such as cattle, rabbits, goats, and pigs. They planted thousands of pine seedlings on the hillsides to support the slowing down of soil erosion.

Irma also plowed patches of soil for neighbors to plant gardens, and she mowed hay. "We made a lot of women mad because I was out in the fields with their husband somewhere," said Irma with a grin. "I usually had someone with me because I didn't trust them either." She even ventured into doing some rudimentary veterinarian work, and extended it to others with animals in the Stinking Creek area.

Irma and Peggy were now shaking off the resistance first shown to them at Stinking Creek.

"Within two years they were asking, 'What creek are you from?,'" noted Irma. "Evidently we were not considered snobs. We had talents which we were willing to share. We'd hear a woman groaning (ready to give birth) and we'd walk in and it would get quiet because they knew Peggy was there."

As the years advanced and new buildings of intentional purpose were built, a multitude of items under the banner "lend-a-hand" became a part of what Irma and Peggy did. They started a 4-H Club for young people, teaching such things as healthier eating and farming activities. They taught Sunday School classes and informally counseled and mentored troubled youth, and at times gave them a place to stay. The operation became a haven for college student volunteers and others with like-minded desires to be of service. The mission of delivering babies was enhanced when Peggy opened a clinic inside the new Center, built in 1965, where many of the other activities are done.

Always a teacher, Irma talked about the way she's

used what she calls "life lessons" to communicate with the young. In discussing Bible teachings, turning abstracts into practical connection in the Stinking Creek community is the goal. Often that means doing chores together and bonding. And with that, she likes using the metaphor of having a "sparkle in your eye" to describe the passion needed to live fully; she likes to demonstrate that in concrete ways. For example, instead of telling one what a "lever" is, they literally move a rock. She relishes lessons to be taught from the daily duties of raising crops and livestock.

And though life at Lend-a-Hand does not move at the frenetic pace it had in the younger days of Irma and Peggy's mission, it still continues to live its name. Irma writes a column for the Barboursville newspaper, *Mountain Advocate,* and Lend-a-Hand is now partnering with the organization, Grow Appalachia, based in Berea, which seeks to help "as many Appalachian families grow as much of their own food as possible." While Irma still lives at her cabin at Lend-a-Hand, she continues to serve and navigates the acreage with her all-terrain vehicle she calls "The Mule." Despite Peggy's diminishing health, she serves as an inspirational spirit.

Certainly, the courageous and tenacious lives of Irma Gall and Peggy Kemner are leaving a legacy of caring in Stinking Creek, a strong foundation, despite the difficulty of their nearly lifelong tasks. To that, Irma states simply: "If you always take the easy way, you won't ever perceive that there's another way."

The source of those words is remarkably credible when she says: "We have always to live our name, Lend-a-Hand."

# Rod Farmer

## *Your Turn*

Overcoming separation,
even isolation,
connecting fragments your
life inevitably bumps into,
creating your own
customized unity,
your particular turn
of life's kaleidoscope,
this personal philosophic
journey is the point
of it all, for us anyway,
not some final destination
some ultimate turn
of the kaleidoscope,
we each get our turn,
so will others in
an infinity of universes,
parallel or otherwise,
so take your turn,
with humility.

# Matthew J. Spireng

## *Us*

I have a photograph taken in 1964
or 1965 of us. You're wearing
a white dress, standing
to my right, smiling. Your
left hand and my right are probably
entwined, though the photo
doesn't show. I'm wearing
a dark suit, smiling so broadly
it's clear I know
I'm the luckiest kid in the world
to be standing so close to a girl
so beautiful, much less her friend,
maybe the boy she loves. The look
on my face defines rapture.
The look on yours is what I love.
I hadn't seen this photograph
in thirty years until I stumbled on it
in my late mother's old album. I
understand why she kept it, just as
I understand why I kept another photo
taken the very same day. It isn't
just a photo of any young couple.
It's a photo of us.

# John P. Kristofco

## *I-80 in Nebraska, going*

coming down from Council Bluffs
to Omaha and Lincoln,
where long, slow breath of August afternoon
spreads out,
the beige and bashful blue
and you,
the voices on the radio
selling clothes and furniture
they won't need since their mother died
and Helen only took one box
to Blair
and where the flat Platte
shifted in its braided path again
and another island disappeared
just like the farms that flickered past,
the homes,
unnoticed like the sandhill cranes,
the coming and the going
of the cars

## *Woodstock (two)*
### 1969


While they gathered up at Yasgur's farm,
another half a million mustered
in the jungles and the paddies
half a world away,
in shelter-halves and holes dug on hillsides
where the angry sun
pressed its unforgiving weight
on shoulders like their uniforms, their duty,
fear;
some arrived by choice,
some stolen from their homes;
some as sure as night and day,
others only certain of the messages of sense
sent along the jagged path of nerve
and blood,
scattered in that church of smoke and death,
teaming of the evening, heat of day,
praying in whatever way they did,
listening to Dylan, Hendrix hymns,
just like all the others,
not as guilty or as innocent
as some would later say,
saints and sinners too,
fable, myth, and history,
My Lai and their sacred marble wall.

# Alden Reimonenq

## *Notch and Raindrop*

Why does it matter
what his hands
marked that night?
Only this desk can recall.

Yet, I lie:
each name
every heart-drawn scratch
etches lovers' moments
into its life
which is long.

In a lifetime
only once or twice
such a moment
lives a lifetime.
He needs this desk
for his notch on mine.

I left no such mark on him.
For, it is hard
to carve yourself
as a raindrop
in a lake.

# Jack Phillips Lowe

## Now And Only Now

Etta pours herself another cup of tea,
sinks into her recliner, tunes in
a rerun of *The Third Man* on TV –
the only program she can find
that's not about sports or Jesus –
and is glad for it.

The annual phone calls
from her kids and grandkids
came and went two hours ago.
Yes, they invited Etta to dinner.
She declined.
Etta can't get around so well anymore.
All those people, the talk and activities –
it's too much for her nerves these days.

Sipping her Earl Grey,
Etta's mind winds back to years past,
when Easter was nothing
but people and activities.
Eggs to color and hide.
Easter baskets to make –
remembering to include the same
number of jelly beans in each one,
so Junior, Britney and Jenna
wouldn't feel slighted.

And of course, the dinner –
so many dinners that Etta captained,
from oven to table to fridge –
ham, mashed potatoes, gravy,

an array of vegetables and bread.
That damned lamb cake she baked every year.
*Nobody* ever ate it.
To think she did all that!
It's almost like it happened to someone else.

Certainly, the people.
One by one, relatives dead and gone,
grown up and moved on,
friends of a dozen and one kinds –
up the block, across the country
or resting now in heaven.
They all stroll past Etta now,
decked out in Easter finery.

This Easter, Etta's house is empty.
Its rooms are silent and its oven, cold.
For decades, Etta thinks,
Easter was really nothing but a to-do list.
Now and only now, she can relax
and savor years' worth of the holiday.
It feels good.

Etta raises her teacup.
"Harry Lime, you're a bastard,"
she says to the TV and settles in
to enjoy the zither music.

## A Phoenix Lurking In Ashes

They just sit there on shelves,
being nothing but party houses
for generations of dust mites.

When they're dead,
they're all utterly and equally dead:
Shakespeare and Neil Simon;
Jane Austen and Jackie Collins;
Charles Bukowski and Rod McKuen.
Posterity neither plays favorites with
nor gives hell to quality and mediocrity –
they're kicked to the curb, just the same.

You know, though, that every book
is a phoenix lurking in ashes.
All it takes is a glance
and suddenly – flame on.
The burning bird is reborn,
glowing with the light and heat of its prime,
even centuries down from its dying day.

And that single spark
is the hope and prayer of every writer
that ever was and ever will be.

# George J. Searles

## *Retirement*

After thirty years or so
he decides to pack it in,
choke down the buffet dinner,
accept the cheap gold wristwatch

and predictably kind words
from friends, quirky relatives,
and co-workers, even those
who didn't really like him.

Then he buys a doublewide
somewhere in the Sunshine State –
Daytona, Port St. Lucie,
or Fort Lauderdale, let's say,

or maybe Sarasota –
and straightaway drops stone dead,
face-first into his salad
(kale, most likely, or quinoa).

Not me. I'll never retire,
and so will live forever.
I'll keep showing up each day,
right here, punching the damned clock.

# Six? I'm Impressed

A lot of the time you can tell who's full
of shit and who's not, but you can never
know with absolute assurance, because,
Hey, it's not always completely clear-cut.

Take Jimmy the cab driver, for instance.
One night at the bar – knowing I write poems –
he bragged, "Poems are fine, but I write *novels*."
"Really, Jim?" I asked, wondering if this

could possibly be true. "Yup," he answered,
downing another bottle of Bud Lite.
"I've written six novels – all pretty good!
Now all I have to do is type them up."

# David Goldstein

## LeRoy's Story

IT WAS A PERFECT DAY for the two hour long trip into the countryside outside Ann Arbor.

Dave Welbourne rubbed his face with sunscreen, put his top down and sped out of town in his new red Fiat. He looked forward to the visit, even if it would take up most of his Saturday.

As he slowed down his car after exiting the expressway he could see the men working the fields, shirts off, lethargic in the sun. The rows of vegetables wouldn't be ready for about a month, maybe more. There was no particular hurry, not here there wasn't. The gates parted for him as he drove inside, pausing only a few seconds to show his identification.

LeRoy hadn't had a visitor for a long time. In fact, a very long time. He was too old to enjoy work in the fields any longer or in the vegetable gardens which would have required some stooping over. Sometimes, though, he strolled aimlessly about outside, not saying much to the younger men. He was always such a calm self-contained old fellow, but, when Dave Welbourne walked in the room, LeRoy rose enthusiastically to greet him. He clasped Dave's hand in both of his and held it. for a full minute. His need of a visitor was apparent. He never had come to grips with his loss and after the initial exchange of greetings, he didn't hesitate to speak about what was always on his mind, an old man with nothing but time to muse.

"I loved that woman so." His old eyes were always rheumy; old man's eyes, he couldn't keep the hint of tears a secret and didn't hardly try to. It had been years now and the tears didn't flow at all anymore; they just seemed to live there always in his eyes on the brink of bursting forth.

"I miss her so.... Oh, well." He stared down at his brown cracked hands. The hands that had managed for himself and then managed for himself and for her as well.

"People, they think I don't understand the woman," he spoke in the present tense. Sometimes he spoke in the past tense and sometimes the present. Maybe the distinction between past and present wasn't all that clear to him anymore.

"I always forgive her. She could always come back. Don't matter what she done. Could always come back here." Did he know where he was? There were times the hands worked two jobs. Sixteen hour days at minimum wage, but he never complained. He looked at his rough old hands . . . fixing on them . . . and then looked up at his visitor. Said matter of factly:

"Black men is made to work. Ain't no gettin' around that one. I never did mind 'bout work. Never did mind 'bout that."

Dave Welbourne put aside his yellow pad and his pen. He looked at the old brown man before him and decided to just spend his Saturday in the country with LeRoy, listening to LeRoy. Did this grandpa of a man have children somewhere, children who visited, or children who never visited? Dave Welbourne did not ask the question.

"She could always come back. Anytime, at all . . . could always come back. She took advantage, I know. When she gone . . . only even a little while . . . I miss her. I do miss her. I tol' her that. No sense playin' the deceiver. I mean what be the point of that?" He put his hand on the visitor's forearm and leaned toward him as though about to confide some great secret, but he spoke out loud without any guardedness at all.

"Price an old man pays for a young thing. I knowed

that from the git-go." He looked in the young white man's eyes and leaned back away from him. Studying him. Making sure he gave his visitor time to think, to learn something, from what he was saying. This old man had learned a little something in his life and he wasn't going to be stingy with it.

"I knew that from the git-go." He chuckled to himself as though he were enjoying the words, or perhaps it was the memory of her he was enjoying as his eyes left his visitor to stare somewhere into the distance. Into the distance or into the past. Where was this old man now? Ten years ago? Five? Three? For certain, longer ago than two; from the satisfaction on his face she was still alive.

"All that running around. I guess she couldn't help it." He appeared on the edge of anger for the briefest moment, but he was maybe too old now to be angry about anything. Anger took a certain amount of energy that probably wasn't worth using. Besides, it could never be said that LeRoy had been what people would call an angry man.

"Forty years old when he decided it was time to take her from me." LeRoy looked up searching the ceiling and shook his head as though barely daring to ask him for some hint, some explanation. "Don't seem fair . . . I mean don't seem fair . . . to her." He shook his head very slowly. "A young woman like that. She don't know nothing 'bout life. I means what's a young woman like that know?"

But LeRoy's visitor wasn't even thirty years old himself. A seventy year old man trying to explain to a thirty year old man what a forty year old woman didn't know about this life. Never would find out. Died young, too young. Dave Welbourne didn't attempt to answer LeRoy's question.

"But she know I loved her. At least she knowed that. Knowed that for sure." The affirmation seemed to make LeRoy feel better. Then he moved somewhere else:

"Played me for a fool, she do."

Dave Welbourne shifted in his straight back metal chair. He could see the men who had earlier been working the fields resting against the trees, trying to stay out of the direct sun during the hottest part of the day. Dave Welbourne loosened his tie. He would soon be sweating lightly. There was no air conditioning inside.

LeRoy sighed. "Ah . . . well." He sat silent for a time. Thinking about her or thinking about whether this young white visitor could possibly understand. Or maybe he was just an old man not thinking anything at all, simply removing himself from all time, the present the past – all time. Maybe just choosing to be comfortable for a part of the time left to him. Enjoying the company of his visitor.

"Guess you can't expect a pretty young gal like that stay home in the house all the day. What? . . . watchin' T.V.? Her . . . not her. She want more from it than that. I don't really blame her. I don't blame her none." In fact, as the doctor's report had described her: She was a 43 year old obese, short, dark-skinned black female. He searched the white man's eyes, then looked away. Could LeRoy read what his visitor was thinking?

"It don't matter. Don't matter at all. I loved her anyway . . . I miss her. I do. Surely I do." He looked down at the floor. "That was one very healthy fine looking young woman."

A rustling began about then and the other visitors in the room began shuffling toward the exit doors, on their way back out into the sunshine. One paused to buy a candy bar from the vending machine. A white man in a drab olive, brown uniform put his hand fondly on LeRoy's shoulder.

"Come on, old man. Time's up."

Dave Welbourne gathered up his yellow pads. He heard the metal door clang behind. LeRoy glanced at his visitor, for the first time looking whipped and broken –

trying to ask his visitor something. Another visit, maybe? Maybe something else.

As he was about to reenter the sunshine for his drive back to Ann Arbor, Dave Welbourne heard the low voice of the man in the drab olive, brown uniform.

"Come on, old boy. Bend over and spread 'em. Sorry about this. No exception. Prison rules."

He'd read the transcript before he came, court assigned to do the appeal . . . if any.

The boyfriend was a heroin dealer. At least the cops were pretty sure about that. She was an addict. On again, off again with the slick neighborhood dude, fifteen years her junior at least. She was found in the white Cadillac with her boyfriend. One bullet in the back of the head. One more for him. And a third for her girlfriend who just happened to be there in the parked car. Close range. All of them. Execution style. Three blocks from home. Her home. LeRoy's home. When the cops arrived at LeRoy's house he still had powder burns on his hands. He hadn't tried to hide the gun. He pointed to the recently fired rifle lying on their bed. He raised no fuss. If he were thirty years younger the judge would have sentenced him to death.

# t. kilgore splake

## amen and hallelujah

dark brautigan creek thicket
moss covered pine stump
jack daniel's bottle
empty tin cup
poem on his lips
holding ticket to ride
loud motherfucking goodbye

## autumn mystery

cold october morning
frost burning off leaves
hiking through wilderness
brook trout fishing
remote beaver dam pond
clouds drifting above
light filtering through foliage
kaleidoscope of different colors
without any wind
grasses ahead moving
small animal disappearing
maybe mountain lion
making quiet escape
or father's ghost
waiting for me

# Anthony G. Herles

## Last Call

GIL WAS CLOSING UP the bar. It was one-thirty, and he had only the bar lights left to turn off when a man came in and sat down on the stool next to the front door. Gil went down the bar and stood opposite the man and said, "Peter Johnson?"

"Nope."

Gil looked closer. "PHS class of '64?"

"Nope."

Gil went back up the bar and returned with a beer and set it down in front of the man. "Dutchess County Chess Champion?"

"Nope."

"Poughkeepsie oarsman of the year in '63?"

"Nope."

"Salutatorian?"

"Nope."

Gil went back up the bar, drew himself a beer, and returned. "Nam veteran?"

The man was silent.

"Well, you look like Peter Johnson to me."

Gil set his beer on the bar. As he moved back, he dropped the bar's cleaning cloth down behind the bar and then he bent down behind the bar to retrieve it. When he stood up, he saw that the other beer was untouched and that the bar was empty.

# Beth Paulson

## On Faith

My father prayed the language of his own,
a deacon in the Methodist church, it was
his voice I heard on Sundays say the words

from the dais where he stood, head bowed
with the minister, other men in dark suits.
Southern Indiana lived in his mouth

even when we moved to the city.
In my Bible his blue ink pen inscribed
my whole name and *Christmas 1953*.

The binding's frayed now, worn by so many
moves more than my use, Can you ever
know what lives in a person's heart?

His later years Dad gave up churchgoing
save for family weddings, a christening,
his second wife not a practitioner of faith.

So we buried his ashes next to his parents,
grassy cemetery plot beside a cornfield
at the edge of his long-ago hometown.

I spoke the eulogy, my language not his own.
The sky was very blue, the corn green, high.
It was hot that July day. I did not cry.

*What follows is the opening chapter of Yard Man, my latest novel from Wings ePress. Yard Man tells the story of Judas Cain, a lonely man simply trying to survive The Great Depression, who suddenly stumbles into a job he doesn't want, falls in love with a prostitute who doesn't love him, and incurs the wrath of the most dangerous man in Mississippi.*

*If you'd like to read the rest of Yard Man, it is available as a paperback or e-book from Wings ePress or Amazon. I hope you enjoy the story of Judas Cain.*

*Chris*

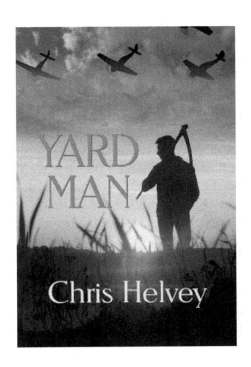

# Chris Helvey

## Book Excerpt: Yard Man

### Chapter 1

IT HAD TO BE THE HOTTEST day of the year. Maybe the decade. Naturally, it was the very day I'd run flat out of coffee and flour and light bread. I'd been out of eggs for a week, but catfish had kept me going. But even they had given up biting in such heat.

My aim had been to wake up before daylight and get moving early, before the worst of the heat. But it had been so hot during the night that it must have been three o'clock before I dozed and when I woke the sun was bright in my eyes. Now it was dead on noon and I was just headed back from A.C. Dupree's Grocery and Meat Market. Sweat covered my face till I looked like the Methodist had baptized me three times and my shirt was stuck to my back. Sweat was even trickling down the crack of my ass, which my Granddaddy Cain, back in Martin County, Kentucky, always said meant a man could quit hoeing and go to the shade for a spell.

Only thing was there wasn't any shade on Evangeline Street and my sack full of groceries felt heavier by the minute. I was glad for my old straw hat, even if it was shot full of holes with the brim plumb broke down.

Otherwise I might have died of heat stroke. Reminded me of forced marches I'd done in the army, and why I'd not bothered to reenlist.

At first I thought I was just hearing voices, on account of the heat, but when they kept up I got to looking around and saw the woman. She was standing on the side porch of a house on the far side of the street. Usually, I don't come home this way – only did this time cause it was so hot and cutting down Evangeline saved me about a quarter mile – and I didn't know her.

I didn't know her and she looked like trouble to me, so I ducked my head and kept walking. Then she started hollering again and when I looked she was waving a handkerchief and making motions like airmen do when they're guiding a plane in.

"You there with the grocery bag, come here for a minute."

I pointed at myself like I wasn't sure she meant me, even though they wasn't any other fool out walking up and down the road under such a broiling sun. No dogs, even. Hell, I might as well have gone and joined up with the French Foreign Legion they're always making movies about. Least then I'd have gotten paid for marching in the midday sun.

Thinking about the midday sun made me think of a poem I'd heard years ago. Something about mad dogs and Englishmen strolling about in the noonday sun. I wasn't up on Englishmen, but I had seen a mad dog once and they plain didn't know what they were doing.

Anyway, the woman nodded and hollered for me to come over and after a few seconds I thought why not. At least I could stand in the shade for a few minutes and maybe she'd let me get a good drink out of her garden hose. So I strolled across the street and up her drive.

It was a big old two story brick place with a garage around back and roses growing in the front. The brick was that shade of yellow that wasn't quite mustard and was real popular down on the Gulf a few years ago in places like Biloxi and Mobile. There was a carport on one end of that house and a covered porch on the other where the woman was standing. At the end of the drive I stepped off and started walking across the grass in front of the house.

Up until last week we'd had plenty of summer rain and the grass was tall and fallen over in spots. Right off I could see the roses needed a good pruning and there was a forsythia bush that had grown up until it was a small jungle. A big limb had fallen off a black oak that grew in front of the bay window and as I stepped over it I wondered if the woman was a widow.

She was standing at the rail, shading her eyes so I couldn't get a good look at her, but I was sure I didn't know the woman. Just guessing, but I'd say she was in her forties, maybe a little over average height for a woman, and starting to put on a few pounds around the middle. She looked down at me over a long nose.

"You one of the Rayburn boys?" she asked. She had a nice voice. Pleasant, with a nice deep throaty sound to it. Sounded like a Mississippi woman to me and that got me to thinking about Annie Curry, which wasn't good for my disposition.

"No, mam. I'm no Rayburn."

"Well you look like one. At least you did when you were on the other side of the street. Are you a Dinkins, then?"

"No, mam. I know a Eudell Denkins, but we're no kin I ever heard tell of."

"Oh my," she said, and I could tell she was all exasperated. She went to fanning herself with a fold of newspaper and I could see a line of sweat above her upper lip.

"Guess you've heard about Henry Lucas?"

"Never heard of him."

"Well, see here now, he was my yard man for better than ten years and then last week he went and had a stroke. In church they tell me. Right while they were singing, 'Leaning On The Everlasting Arms'."

"That's one of my favorite hymns," I said and went to singing the chorus, "Leaning, leaning, leaning on the everlasting arms, Leaning..."

"Hush up there, you. Hush up right this minute. I didn't call you over to hear you sing. Besides you sure don't have much of a voice."

"Reckon I can sing alright, mam. It's just carrying the tune along that I never was real good at."

"Oh, for pity's sake, hush."

I shut my mouth then and shifted my groceries to the other arm and looked up into the woman's nostrils. She had a good enough nose, nice and straight, just bigger than most women's. Not that such a thing bothered me at all. Not with mine having been broke three times. No, I'm sure not a pretty sight. Oh, I'm not some monster. But, on the other hand, Hollywood studios aren't beating a path to my shack with a contract in their hands. Anyway, I didn't say anything more right then. Learned a long time ago not to aggravate a woman with money, and if she lived on this street she had money. Or her husband did.

"What I'm trying to find out is whether you know a man who can cut our grass." She nibbled on her lower lip, looking something like a giant rabbit, and said "And it needs to be cut today. Tomorrow, as you surely know, is the Fourth of July and my husband and I are having a party. And as you can see, what with Henry dying and all, it was really a most inconvenient time for him to pass, the yard looks awful and some of the women are coming from my Sunday School class. We're Methodists, you know. And I will just curl up and die if they see the place looking like this." She gave me a pleading look and then sighed deeply.

Now I hadn't even realized it was coming up on Independence Day – a man living by himself doesn't pay much heed to holidays, one day being so much like another – and I sure didn't give a diddly about a bunch of Methodist women, but for some reason I did feel sorta sorry for that woman. Maybe it was cause her nose was a little big, or maybe it was because she looked soft around the middle, like her body and her life were both getting away from her. Or maybe it was because she had this look on her face like she'd lost her way and didn't have the first idea about how to get back on the path.

Anyway, I could see that it was going to be a long afternoon, but I was durned if I was going to just up and be a Good Samaritan, even if that person was about my favorite person in the whole Bible. Old and New Testaments, saving Jesus, of course, who really wasn't actually a person. Not really. What he actually was, when you got down to the truth, was God, which just thinking about always gave me a headache. God and Jesus were both beyond my powers of understanding. However, I did have a feeling for the old Holy Ghost. Maybe cause I was sort of like a ghost myself, slipping in and then out of people's lives. People are alright, but for me they were sorta like castor oil. Meaning, naturally, that I could only take them in small doses.

Sweat felt heavy on my forehead and I tugged out my sweat rag and swiped it across my face. "Guess I could mow it for you," I said and gave her a look out of the corners of my eyes. "That is, if the pay is right."

"Oh," she said, "oh. My husband always paid Henry and I'm not sure what he paid him." She dabbed at her checks with a lace hanky. "Would a dollar be enough?"

"Well," I said, drawing the word out and letting it hang out there in the air like a punted football.

"Two?" She sounded half cross and half desperate.

"I generally get three dollars when I mow a big yard like this." Now that wasn't a lie. One time I'd mowed around the graves for the Baptist and they'd given me three dollars. Course, they probably figured it was missionary money, but it spent just the same.

"Can you start now, Mr. ...er, I'm afraid I don't

know your name." She sighed again and seemed to sag in on herself. Her prominent bosom positively drooped, putting me in mind of a big sunflower starting to wilt.

"It's powerful hot, but seeing as how you're in a bind I'll get started. You can just call me Judas. My full name is Judas Cain."

"Oh my," she said. "What an unusual name. I'm Mrs. Arthur Ayers." She swallowed and smiled. It was a phony smile, but then she wasn't having a particularly good day.

"The lawn mower is in the shed out back. You should be able to find it easily. The shed's unlocked, Mr. Cain. You can leave your groceries in there while you mow."

Suddenly, she clapped her hands and her eyes got big like a bee had gone up her dress. "Oh, I must go now. My husband will be home any minute and he'll want his lunch. I must go. You can handle things from here?"

"Can I have a drink of water before I start? I'm powerful thirsty."

She gave me a hard look and I could tell she was anxious for me to get mowing. Still, I was thirsty and the air was oven hot.

"Surely you wouldn't want another yard man to have a stroke." I grinned real big like we were old fishing buddies. "Neighbors might start to talk, you know."

She looked like she was about ready to have a stroke herself, or maybe simply melt into a pool of butter like those lions or tigers or whatever wild beast was in the Little Black Sambo books. Her throat worked some like she was trying to swallow a big lump. Finally she got it down.

"There's a garden hose right over there. Help yourself."

# Stephanie Hiteshew

## *They were at the counter*


and you were saying something
about your father's farm and
the horse he bought you when you
were just a child, along with a cow girl
outfit to match –
sticks started the fires only
to scare the people with badges
(who took her brother away)
and the barn shot, like a junkie,
up in flames, collapsing the fences
as you stood there, staring –
        horses running free
you: in pajamas, and rubbing
your eyes, while others believing,
this little girl needs to sleep;
but not me, I'm accustomed
to the scent of gasoline. We
were at the counter and they didn't
even notice.

# Blair Ewing

## Shanghai Husband

Turns out I've always been
    a good Shanghai husband,
man enough to carry my wife's purse
    like a halfback juking
in the open field.
    I may be weak enough to kill you
but I'm strong enough to yield.

# *Parker Towle*

## *Mother*

She was born at home where vast fields
sweep down to the Miller River. As a child
she slept with nesting mice. The farmhouse
watched over aromatic grass and milk
flowed in the barns. She stared
into the eyes of cows and was satisfied.
Riding high on a hay wagon or bundled
in skins on a horse drawn sleigh
she ruled, she says, her father's favorite.

His kidneys failing, eyelids puffed
and grayed, she was swelling too; and
as his movements stilled and stopped
her son flexed in her womb and thumped
against her belly wall. In one

room in his homestead on the pond
she wondered, Christmas candles lit,
nineteen thirty-three, husband
depression-logging deep
in timber blowdowns, if
dust out west would dampen
in a wet recovery. She nursed her child.

# Eric Greinke

# The Seminal Ginsberg

LIKE HIS IMMEDIATE PREDECESSOR and greatest
influence Walt Whitman, Allen Ginsberg was a seminal,
universal poet. Ginsberg's seminality was of a different
kind than Whitman's, however. Both poets had similar
approaches and world views, but their influence was
different largely due to historical/cultural context.

So much has already been written about Ginsberg's
life and work that it would be redundant of me to repeat
it here. Instead, my goal is to point out those aspects of
his that characterize the universal poet. If I had to
describe Ginsberg in two words, I'd use "open" and
"expansive." He drew his strength from an ever-
expanding ego that identified with humanity.

There is little doubt that Ginsberg had a profound
influence on both American and international literature.
He consciously adapted the world view and methods of
Whitman, acknowledged in excerpts from one of his last
collections, *Cosmopolitan Greetings – Poems 1986-
1992*:

I write poetry because Walt Whitman gave world
  permission to speak
with candor.

I write poetry because Walt Whitman opened up
  poetry's verse-line for
unobstructed breath.

\* \* \*

I write poetry to talk back to Whitman, young people
  in ten years, talk
to old aunts and uncles still living near Newark, New
  Jersey.

* * *

I write poetry because Chuang-tzu couldn't tell
  whether he was butterfly or man, Lao-tzu said
  water flows downhill, Confucius said
honor elders, I wanted to honor Whitman.

* * *

I write poetry because Walt Whitman said, "Do I
  contradict myself?
Very well then I contradict myself (I am large, I
  contain multitudes.)"

Allen Ginsberg,
from *Improvisation in Beijing*

Ginsberg departs from Whitman in his lifelong
devotion to other poets whom he admired. He was adept
at promotion like Whitman, but he focused it more on
promoting the work of others than Whitman did. Few of
these poets had Ginsberg's energy or talent, but that
never seemed to bother him. Many of these poets would
not have come to widespread recognition had they not
been associated with Ginsberg, but beyond that,
Ginsberg himself wouldn't have been as recognizable if
he wasn't (along with the reluctant Jack Kerouac) the
leader of a literary *and* social movement. Indeed, his
influence on society went far beyond literature.

His humanistic perspective had its roots in the ideas
of his parents. His mother was a Marxist and his father
a poet/schoolteacher. He came from a family of Russian
Jews who were politically active and humanistically

oriented.

Ginsberg was influenced by Kerouac more than any other peer. Kerouac's theory that the "first thought is the best thought" intrigued Ginsberg, who frequently attempted to write spontaneously, seldom with the success of his longer, carefully wrought early poems like *Howl* and *Kaddish*. When he was spontaneous, he was often silly. He wrote poems that were simple rhymes, often single-layered, humorous or even sarcastic. Like Whitman, Ginsberg's best poems were long-lined barrages of imagery and direct, declarative statement. But, his shorter, more spontaneous poems (again like Whitman) reveal a more personal side of him. For all his campaigning, he still tried not to take himself too seriously.

Like Whitman, Ginsberg wasn't accepted by the academy or the established literati until after he became the most popular poet in America. Like Whitman, he took his case directly to the people.

The "beatnik" phenomena, which began in the fifties in the bohemian Greenwich Village of New York City and quickly spread to San Francisco's North Beach, deeply affected the post-war baby boomers and transmogrified into the hippie youth culture of the sixties that produced major paradigm changes in music, politics, race relations and social values. Allen Ginsberg was a seminal figure in all of it, going far beyond the norm for the influence of any other poet of his time or of poets in general. His openness about his sexuality foreshadowed the gender pride movement of today, and he asserted that the role of the poet should be to influence mankind toward greater tolerance and altruism.

Significantly, the Beatniks entered the consciousness of the baby boom generation before the literary Beats. I was in Junior High School (AKA "Middle School") when a half-hour sitcom, *Dobie Gillis*, captured the imaginations of adolescents with its

Beatnik character Maynard G. Krebs (played by Bob Denver). Maynard had a chin beard, wore a black sweater with the sleeves pushed up and sneakers. He played a bongo drum and used hip jargon. He called everyone "man" and objected to work of any kind with a loud "Work!" He was the perfect cartoon Beatnik and completely stole the show from the main character. It wasn't long before a small group of the more creative kids at my school began playing the bongo drums, talking and dressing like Maynard G. Krebs. When high school came the next year, phase two began.

Some of us were into reading and writing, and the fun of the Beatnik thing morphed us into receptors for the literary Beats. A group of us used to go into the city often, making the rounds of the bookstores, going to the Art Museum (which had no entry fee then) and identifying as budding Bohemian artist types. The boys grew sparse chin beards and the girls had long, straight hair. Both wore black almost exclusively. On one such excursion, I bought a trade paperback, *The Beats*, an anthology edited by Seymour Krim. This book proved to be the final piece of the puzzle. Writers weren't bookish nerds as we had gathered from the sneers of our more conformist peers, they were cool! Especially the one named Allen Ginsberg. He was the quintessential Beat, and he captured our attention like no other. Then we read *Howl*.

The worldwide effect of *Howl* alone would quality Ginsberg as a great poet. But he did much more than that. He inspired a generation to transcend convention and conformity. Ginsberg told us it was okay, even admirable, to forge your own trail. This is the message that made him the most influential poet of his time.

Sure, the *Life Magazine* article featuring Ginsberg's performance of *Howl* in San Francisco's Gallery Six had already been published, alerting the adults, but we baby boomers were early teens. We didn't read *Life Magazine*. But we watched *Dobie Gillis*.

Maynard G. Krebs led us to Allen Ginsberg. While this may seem like a tenuous and even superficial premise, I know that this was indeed the route for the post-war generation that eventually became hippies. The social contagion was first, and those of us with a literary bent combined the influences. I believe my experience to be representational because I was born in 1948, which was the big bump of the baby boom, with more people born than any other year of that period. Ginsberg was always a pop star. His popularity opened the way for his poetry, and for that of numerous others of his own generation and those to follow.

Like Whitman before him, Ginsberg's approach had wide popular appeal because it emphasized social content that related to real people and was not decorous or obscure, but relied instead on strong rhythm, repetition and direct, declarative statements.

It is well known that Ginsberg worked diligently his whole life to promote himself, a wide variety of other writers and a large number of social causes. Like Whitman, he firmly believed that the role of the poet goes far beyond the merely literary. His ego was expansive and, like the confessionalists, he felt strongly that openness and candor have both cathartic and healing value. *Kaddish* is the greatest "confessional poem" ever written, far superior to anything by Lowell, Plath, Snodgrass or Olds because it is also a complex love poem. The poem is more about his mother than him.

By the time of the Gallery Six reading which debuted *Howl* to the world, he had already begun connecting with other avant garde poetry scenes. The Beat movement began in New York's Greenwich Village, expanded to San Francisco's North Beach, and quickly spread throughout the major cities of America. Ginsberg's purpose (and sense of humor, greater than Whitman's) had already been broadcasted in his famous early poem *America*:

America you don't really want to go to war.
America it's them bad Russians.
Them Russians them Russians and them Chinamen.
And them Russians.
The Russia wants to eat us alive. The Russia's power
    mad. She wants to take our cars from out our
    garages.
Her wants to grab Chicago. Her needs a Red *Reader's*
    *Digest*. Her wants our auto plants in Siberia. Him
    big bureaucracy running our filling stations.
That no good. Ugh. Him make Indians learn read. Him
    need big black niggers. Hah. Her make us all work
    sixteen hours a day. Help.
America this is quite serious.
America this is the impression I get from looking in
    the television set.
America is this correct?
I'd better get right down to the job.
It's true I don't want to join the Army or turn lathes in
    precision parts factories, I'm nearsighted and
    psychopathic anyway.
America I'm putting my queer shoulder to the wheel.

from *America*


    My first direct experience of Ginsberg came in
1972, when he was a featured poet at the 2nd National
Poetry Festival sponsored by my alma mater Grand
Valley State University. I was asked to give a reading
on one of the evenings of the week-long event, and
Ginsberg was in the audience three rows back to my left.
I couldn't take my eyes off him and I'm afraid I read
almost exclusively directly to him. He smiled his
encouragement throughout, and I can still see his face
clearly in my memory. There were a number of famous

poets in that audience, but I had eyes only for him because I was so impressed with his poetic/social act to that date. He exuded unmistakable warmth and charisma. When he entered a room, all eyes were on him.

The next time I saw him (also at GVSU a few years later), I attended a workshop he gave. We sat on the floor in a circle and Allen led us in chanting Om.

The last time I saw him, in the late seventies, he played his little harmonium and sang his original blues songs. I remember that his rhythm was good and his singing was a cross between dramatic speech and enthusiastic screech. By then he traveled with an entourage that included Peter Orlovsky and several others. He was a bona fide pop star.

Ginsberg was very impressed with Bob Dylan and developed a relationship with the great poet/musician. I think his development of blues songs and the use of the little harmonium during the final phase of his poetry was mainly inspired by Bob Dylan's success melding poetry and music (for which Dylan eventually won the Nobel Prize). Ginsberg wanted, above all, to *spread the word*, and he saw music as a means to that end.

Ginsberg didn't care much about having an original style. He was deeply interested in the Big Picture issues of poetry, such as freedom of speech, equal rights extending beyond political borders, open mindedness, tolerance and spirituality. Ginsberg's personal style reflected his many changing moods and enthusiasms. Although he is not known for his subtlety, there is a subtle, ironic sense of humor that runs through his various approaches to style as a common thread. He understood that style is a superficial difference between poets, but content (and its moral implications) is the fundamental value of poetry. Styles vary, even within the work of one writer. The original Beats (Kerouac, Burroughs, Corso, Di Prima, Ferlinghetti, et al.) had little in common on a stylistic level except a tendency toward the first person autobiographical persona, but they shared a belief in personal freedom and open-minded tolerance of others.

He also worked toward mutual understanding between diverse schools of thinking. He knew that the potential of poetry is large enough to "contain multitudes" (Whitman). New York School poets, Black Mountain poets, Deep Imagists, West Coast Meat/Street poets and Language poets were all accepted, promoted and socially connected by Ginsberg, who maintained an extensive mailing list of poets, editors and artists of every leaning. It was poetry itself that Ginsberg championed, and this is a major trait of a true universal poet.

Ginsberg was able to reconcile their wide range of literary approaches, from the spontaneous bop prosody of Kerouac to the cut-ups of Burroughs to the mythological/archetypal breath units of Di Prima, all under one "movement" based on primarily an *attitude.* That attitude, that "anything goes," was to become so integrated into poetic practice that it is now on an assumptive level. Ginsberg appreciated the enormous resource that diversity brings to poetry (and life). His defense of democratic values was at least as great as Whitman's. The nature of Ginsberg's seminality was that he influenced others to 'be themselves' in their lives and art. He was a one-man Liberation Front.

Above all Ginsberg was a poet of ideas/ideals. He worked with various borrowed styles because content was his priority. He had this in common with Whitman, whose styles *were* original and innovative, but for whom content was also paramount. Both poets achieved universality primarily through the strength of their democratic ideas. Both conceptualized poetry as an instrument of social progress.

Content is the key to Ginsberg's seminality. If it was based on style, *he wouldn't have been significant at all.* But as a social activist who used poetry as a means of social change, Ginsberg was highly significant and influential.

The elevation of substance over surface is the very essence of a universal poet. Is it any wonder that Whitman and Ginsberg are the two American poets who have achieved the greatest international recognition? Ideas transcend the smoke and mirrors of simple style as evidenced by their greater translatability into other languages. Universal human truths are more powerful than mere cultural differences and pass through border walls as if they are built of mist.

Sources

*Cosmopolitan Greetings – Poems 1986-1992;* Allen Ginsberg; Harper Perennial; New York, NY; 1995.

*Selected Poems 1947-1995;* Allen Ginsberg; Perennial Classics; New York, NY; 1996.

*The Beats*; Seymour Krim; Fawcett Publications, Inc; Robbinsdale, MN; 1960.

# D.L. Tickel

## *Night School*

Drunks are assholes,
Scary keeping you awake
Into the morning,
Removing Walt Whitman doors from
Broken jambs
Almost blasting themselves with
Frankenstein electricity. Are you jealous,
Charles Bukowski?

My
Father's mother, only fifty nine when she
Was struck like Julia, John Lennon's mom.
Dad should've cried at
Grandma's funeral; it
Might've helped.

My parents
Battled
When they were drunk, because
Mom's parents
Only lived three hours away, because
Dad, who played basketball,
Always got in the ref's face. Dad gave Mom
Only one black eye.

I'd have to get
Out of bed, but I didn't have to play piano
For a buncha losers like the young Beethoven.
My kid sister
Would hang on to my slingshot as I went downstairs
To dad who would

Smile proudly at me, his only son, while
Sobbing intelligibly, criticizing
Red AM and blue FM, clumsily scratching
Jim Croce's Life & Times. Country was country.
Instrumentalists played to a
4/4 beat. Bells
Were not tubular.

Odds were Dad,
Who remained an occasional marathoner,
Wouldn't make it to work, but like he said,
After he retired, he "never missed a paycheck."
And Mom, who became a nightly sprinter,
Who liked show tunes, sappy (The Air That I Breathe)
And senseless (Whiter Shade of Pale) pop,
Never missed a day with her third graders.

# Bernadine Fillmore

## Prison Release

I'm coming out today, on prison release.
You're doing time, what are you in for
Being black and at a disadvantage.

Can't afford a quiet place
Government has made sure of that
Out on Prison Release, really only temporary that's
what I call
living in public housing.

Dope addicts, drunken, women selling their bodies, for
a five-dollar bag
Children running wild, Seniors have to.
People with jobs feel that they deserve better
treatment.
Make No Difference on Prison Release.

Living in a Danger Zone.

Government says you could be homeless.
we're giving them a place to stay.
We all are living here together, and are out on
Prison Release.

# R.T. Castleberry

## *This Trace of Serenity*

I've spent the hours
watching overflights of airliners,
choppers bank low, in line
with hospital spires.
Blue jay and robin dart
from oaks to feeding field.
A grey calico cat makes
his run across cracked tarmac,
tail flicking through a broken fence.
A spoiling cloud builds to the west.
The day seems a haiku
of mechanics and the wild.

# Mark Havlik

## Almost a Life

I AM STANDING STONE-STILL on the front porch of an elegant full-bricked Brooklyn home. My eyes clamped on the diamond-shaped cutout bulging from the top half of a door adorned with shards of painted-glass. Its bell lit half-heartedly in a somber yellow barely visible lies below. I was here a month ago, a year ago. Never pressed it; walked away. But on this dark, dank Friday's night entombed in late fall, the world reeking of decay, veiled in hopelessness with spring an eternity away, I am so emptied the weight is more than I can bear. So I raise my finger and hear the ringing echo inside. A sound not unfamiliar to my ears, though tonight the noise is so fiercely unsettling, the nerves in my lower limbs spark, then ignite. My legs are cranked up to flee and my frail body is twisting about. It is all I can do to anchor myself by holding on tightly to the door knob until I feel it turning.

It is Nathan's hand turning the knob. I know this because when the door sweeps open I hear his voice. "Matthew, Matthew," he cries out in the same harmonious tone he has always used whenever he greets me, even the first time, when he was Mr. Chernoff, and I was collecting his darling, dazzling daughter Melanie for a date. I think he liked the sound of my name, or maybe what he enjoyed more was how he sounded when he said it. Perhaps, a little of both. Although Melanie once told me it was more likely the latter. Could be she was right, but I will never know for sure.

"Matthew, Matthew," he says again then ushers me in, closes the door and stares at me until he realizes he is doing just that. "You're back. Finally, you've come back to us. We've been waiting." Nathan is a good soul. He doesn't ask why. He can't. Besides, he saw the answer when he set his eyes upon me – the aura of that red-raw scar seared into my uneasy gaunt face. He is floundering I can tell, so I toss him a lifeline. It is the least I can do, though it surprises me I can do as much as that.

"Is Sophie home?" I ask.

"Of course, of course. What's the matter with me? She's in the kitchen." He calls for her but hears nothing. "She must be doing the dishes. Let me get her. Come in, come in," he beckons as he darts down the hallway in search of his much needed wife.

But I don't. I stay in the hallway, slide over to the staircase pinned to the wall; put my hand atop the flawlessly-smooth, rounded finial of the last baluster on the landing. My head angles up, higher and higher, following each step and riser from bottom to top, though the rest of me is held below in the uncompromising grip of gravity. It will not accommodate as it so often did when it would graciously give way then watch in wonderment as Melanie and I flew up the stairs with hearts and hands bound together. Now such a daunting, distant past it lingers lightly in my tremulous grasp.

"Matthew, my dear son," Sophie says as she closes in on me, her arms full out and open. I don't, but I sense Nathan blanch when he hears his wife call me "son." Her almond-shaped eyes moisten to the margin as she hugs me; her tongue unnaturally knotted she cannot speak another word so she keeps me in her clutches and I can't break free until Nathan repays a favor.

"Enough already, Sophie. The poor boy can't breathe."

She steps back, unabashed, and with an uncoiled tongue says what Nathan dared not. "It's been nearly a year and a half since we saw you. We love you, Matthew. You're part of this family. Isn't that right, honey?"

Nathan nods. My fingers burrow into the finial. Sophie goes on.

"Why haven't you come sooner? Even if only to say hello and visit a few minutes."

"I didn't want to disturb," I answer as my gaze pivots from her to the top stair.

And I see what lies around the turn – the pleasure palace awash in shimmering blues and ethereal white, where once the moon full passed through arched windows bowed and beamed us a smile. The kingdom I am driven mad to reclaim in all its glory. Alas, I cannot, for it has melted into the mist, morphed into legend, what was our Camelot.

Sophie takes another step back. I know what she is going to say before the words stand blade-straight in her mind. It is what everyone tells me, though there is so much more compassion when she speaks her voice and more than that mimic what comes out her mouth. "You look *so* exhausted, Matthew." Her head drops in the next instant. She has lost the strength to keep it level and can no longer look at me. I understand. I never look, either. There are no mirrors in my apartment. I ripped them out two years ago.

"Come into the living room, Matthew," Nathan offers. "We can sit, talk. Sophie will brew us some coffee. We have cheesecake, the kind you like." I shake my head. "For a little while," Nathan pleads, his hand on my shoulder trying to nudge me along. But the finial and I are inseparable.

Sophie revived draws near. Places a tap-water warm hand on my sallow cheek. "You don't sleep much."

Hardly a question, yet I answer as if it is. "I sleep enough," I tell her. Another lie pouring from my pale, parched lips, but it slips by without rebuke.

Instead, she turns to her husband muttering, "Coffee, coffee. You want him to stay up all night. Look at him!"

Yes, look. But without my precious Melanie what is there to see of me?

# Cathy Porter

## *No Trail*

In one dream, you never
correct me – let me flounder
in a sea of grammatical errors;
make messes, spill drinks
all over the couch.

In another, you fall off a cliff,
land in a field of pillows
covered in roses, bring me a dozen.

I wake to find the eyes of summer
closing. You leave soon after,
no trail left behind.

The 10 o'clock streetlight
blinks reds 'till dawn. Small town
curfew.

Dreams of money and security –
dreams of blue skies and eternal sun.
Every dream on a silver platter –
and yet, you still walk away.

# Are We Great Yet?

My neighbor's dog jumped his fence
the other day and took off running.

Across the city, on the west side,
the neighbors are shocked that a string
of cars have been broken into:

"This just doesn't happen here!"

These winter months bring out
the cold in too many hearts. Sends people
to the streets in acts of desperation.

Sara and Scott were kicked out of the bar
for pissing in each other's drinks.
Just like the government.

They still haven't found my neighbor's dog.
He was last seen trying to jump over
a higher fence down the road –
probably to get inside a warm house
for a bite to eat.

I don't know his name, but it doesn't matter –
nothing does, when you're scared and hungry.

# Robert Ronnow

## *Chainsaw Certified*

I'm dead. Unlike Frost and Yeats
nothing I've said will be remembered.
Unlike Roosevelt and Lincoln
nothing I'm thinking will win the war.

I'm going to go to my grave unsung
like almost everyone. These mountains
are my grave. A good grave
to go to. There's no such thing

as being saved. When you're gone
you're done. At least 60 million
people don't believe it, don't believe
in evolution. Man, that ape,

can heap a peck of hurt posthaste
with earth movers and machine guns.
Information technology
cannot save your soul, heck,

I've tried. Every morning
I total the polloi
coming to my site for wisdom.
The number's usually zero.

A good number to know.
When my heart fibrillates
I lay my head
against my sleeping wife.

Solace, comfort. She says,

Take your pill, fool.
In an hour at most
I'm feeling great again!

# J.S. Kierland

# An Unexpected Challenge

*(A novel-in-progress excerpt)*

EVER SINCE WILLY TWO HORSE had been elected as the Tupai Tribe's President its board meetings kept getting closer and closer to the designated starting time of two o'clock. The latest meeting got underway at 2:37 p.m., less than an hour late and the closest it had ever been to starting on time. Only the tribal Secretary, Willy's niece, seemed to notice this growing achievement and she gave her uncle a big smile as he brought down the gavel to start another Wednesday board meeting. "Lots of business to cover today," Willy stated. "If needed, we will discuss and vote on old business after the Secretary reads the minutes from our last meeting."

Viola smiled attentively and began reading her notes in a clear and resonant voice. "The last meeting opened with a short discussion on designated parking for board members and was tabled for future discussion by President Two Horse. The next order of business was raising the board's salaries. The President tabled that as well. Estimated costs for soil testing at the new casino site were asked for, but the study was not completed. There was no new business," Viola said, smiling at her uncle and putting the shorthand pad down on the table, then placing her pen neatly over it.

Willy nodded his approval and with a sharp crack of his new gavel, he announced, "Old business is open for discussion."

Suzie blurted, "I'd like to discuss all this stuff in the

papers about the Lee Boys, sir."

It was the first time anyone in the room had referred to Willy as 'sir,' and it brought about an immediate silence rather than the usual argument over the motion itself. All eyes looked to Willy, and he said, "That's not old business, Suzie."

"But it is, sir. You were the one that mentioned we should be ready for those guys to come and ask for a loan."

Willy nodded and said, "That's a good point, Suzie. Have you anything to add?"

Willy's agreeable answer caught Suzie by surprise and she looked around the room at the faces staring back at her before saying, with an uncertain shrug, "I just wondered if anyone knew what was going on with them?"

"I'd like to know that myself," Nelson added.

"Aren't they your friends?" Suzie asked.

"I don't think so," Nelson replied defensively.

"I noticed *your* picture in the *Courier*, sir," Tanya said. "You were at Mr. Lee's funeral."

"Jim was my friend. We worked together many years."

They waited expectantly for Willy to continue and explain the entire situation in detail, which was the one thing he was trying to avoid. He stared back at them and said, "All I know is that Mr. Lee was very ill."

"The guys down at the barber shop – "

"Be careful what you say here, Nelson," Willy warned. "Everything in this room is legally binding and we don't want to involve the Tribe in any way, do we?" Viola wrote furiously in her shorthand and Willy said, "I think you better leave all this out of the minutes, dear," and Nelson sat back in his chair satisfied with Willy's suggestion of avoiding the subject.

"Are they coming for a loan, or not?" Suzie asked.

"I don't know," Willy told her, but he could see they were expecting a lot more because he was the only one in the room who'd actually been at Jim Lee's funeral. "I really don't know anymore than you do about this," he went on, looking into each face around the table. "And I don't *want* to know anymore than you do," he added. A chorus of grunts and groans followed and Willy searched their expectant faces, looking to see if any of them actually believed what he'd just told them. Only the Doubting Nelson looked like he hadn't quite accepted it, but that was usual with Nelson so Willy let it ride and said, "The next old business is the soil testing results and cost estimates for the proposed new casino."

"I have that, sir," Tanya said, waving a batch of papers in her hand and offering them to Willy.

"You can present it," Willy said with a smile.

His quick comment surprised Tanya, and she cleared her throat, faced the table, and said, "Well, the only thing in this report that really matters is that the soil at the proposed building site can *not* hold up a large building. In fact, it really can't hold up much at all," she said, checking her notes. "Maybe a gas station if it doesn't get too busy," she mumbled, looked around the table at the shocked faces, and said, "In other words, if we wanted to build on that spot we'd have to reinforce the soil and that would cost an extra fifty million, at least," she said, checking her notes again.

"Dollars?" Suzie piped, and Tanya nodded.

"And that's just for starters," Nelson said.

"A new hotel and casino would cost much more than that," Tanya grunted, and sat back down in the deafening silence.

"Are there any other suggestions?" Willy asked.

"It was a dumb idea anyway," Nelson grunted.

The women's hands went up and Willy said quickly, "We won't get anywhere arguing over the facts. We either vote to 'fix' the site or drop it." The hands began to wave. "I suggest we think long and hard about this before making any kind of a decision. I'll have the architecture firm present their findings in person, and explain the entire situation in detail before you vote on it."

"Thank you, sir," Tanya said, and the hands went down.

"Any new business?"

"Can we talk about the new casino?" Suzie squeaked.

"The new casino is now old business," Willy said, glancing around the room. No one moved. "I have an announcement," he said. "I'm going on short exploratory trips to other tribes in the area, and might miss some meetings, but Nelson can handle things here."

The women in the room made quick, uncertain glances to each other and Nelson asked, "How long will you be gone?"

"I don't know, but you can always get me on the phone or the computer if you need a tie breaking vote," Willy said, and a muttered agreement went around the table. "Are there any new motions?" Silence. "Motion to end the meeting?" Mrs. Buford raised her hand, Nelson seconded, chairs scraped, and the board members headed for the door.

"Will you be gone long?" Viola asked, gathering her notepad and pen.

"A few short trips, but there's something I'd like to discuss with you before I go. Let's talk in my office," he said, and they moved out into the hall behind the others.

"I'll make some fresh coffee," Viola piped.

"I'm trying to cut back," Willy muttered.

"Oh, then I'll just take what's left."

Willy went into the office and sat behind the old desk, and tried to formulate what he would say to her and how he would say it. He'd been close to Viola, particularly after his brother's sudden death. They had actually taken Viola in like a third daughter after his brother's accident. Viola and her brother celebrated birthdays with them and knew their secrets and problems as if his brother was still there with them. The adjustment had been harder for Viola's mother, but after years of mourning she'd become part of the extended family too, and more and more dependent on his advice and guidance. They'd all become close and Willy had been careful not to mention this new situation to anyone, not even his wife, and wondered what his brother would have done if he were alive.

Willy heard Viola's heels clicking toward him, grabbed the tissue box out of the bottom drawer, and, just as he was placing it up on the desk, Viola came in and put her teddy bear coffee mug down next to it.

"Do you have a cold, Uncle Willy?" she asked.

"Just some allergies," he lied. "Maybe you better close the door." Viola hesitated, closed the door and sat down. "I don't have much time, and wanted to clear up a few things before I leave tomorrow," he lied again.

"You're going to fire me, aren't you?" she asked, reaching for a tissue. "I knew it was coming," she sobbed. "I just don't understand why they jumble all those letters on the keyboard? It makes spelling harder. Why don't they just put them in the right order?" she blurted, blowing her nose and snapping out another set of tissues with her long flaming red fingernails. "I know you try to help me – "

"No one is going to fire you," Willy said.

"They all say I'm not very good."

"You've been secretary for so many chiefs – "

"That's true, but none of them were smart like you."

"I'm not firing you!" he said, raising his voice.

By then her eye makeup smeared and she gave him a half-smile from behind the tissues, and said, "You're not?"

"Why would I do that?"

"Because I can't – "

"There's something else...much more serious."

"More serious than getting fired?" she asked in astonishment and grabbed another tissue.

This wasn't the way he'd planned. He was off to a bad start and began to realize there was no easy way to bring a subject like this to the surface, especially with someone young and fragile like Viola.

"I'm concerned – "

"I hope you haven't told anyone else about it," she interrupted from behind the tissues.

"No, I'd never do that. I'm just concerned – "

"That dumb bird told you, didn't he? The one they call, Coco...Coocoo...or whatever his name is."

"Coocochee...you know him?"

"Know him? Every time I look up...he's there." She started sobbing again and Willy pushed the box of tissues closer. She snapped up several in a row.

Willy had expected tears but not this. He started to say, "Things are going to be all right," but couldn't move his mouth and he just sat there trying not to notice the distress Viola had fallen into. He finally got up, went around the desk, knelt down next to her, and said, "You've got to break it off with him." She began to cry even harder and louder. "I'm only trying to help," he pleaded. "We can do this together. The others don't have to know."

"You're making it worse," she said, peeking out from behind the tissues. "I thought you were going to fire me because I can't type," she said. "But this?" Her dark wet eyes grew larger and she stared back at him. "You've been spying on me with that damn Raven!"

Willy hesitated, then tried to get up. Viola rose in the chair and stepped away from him. "I just don't want it to become serious," he said, looking up at her. "I'm sure your mom doesn't either. You're just a young girl – "

"No one knows about it," she said. "Except you!" Willy grabbed the arm of the chair and tried to raise himself up. "It's all because some Coocoo bird saw us through the window," she snapped. "It's nobody's business!"

"You're having an affair with a tribal board member!"

"I don't care what he is. You just tell that bird to stop flying around and peeking in windows!"

"No, I meant the vice-president, Nelson...*he's* the vice-president and he's married."

"What's that got to do with me?"

"What about his wife?"

"That's her problem...not mine! She doesn't care. She's into drugs!"

"Did Nelson tell you that?"

"That's none of *your* business."

Willy staggered back behind his desk, stretched his cramped leg, and blurted, "Nelson's wife is sick and takes medicines."

"Bullshit! She buys her pills from my brother."

"Rudy sells drugs?"

"She's such a good customer he gives her a discount!"

"But Rudy's still in high school!"

"How old do you have to be to sell drugs in this country?" she snapped, grabbing another handful of tissues. "Rudy's been selling drugs for years. That's what he does, like the kids in the hood."

"Hood?"

"Baltimore and LA...y'know, those guys with cell phones. Don't you watch TV?"

Willy shook his head. "Winona watches it," he mumbled.

"An she talks to birds too...right?"

"Not anymore," Willy snapped.

Viola kept throwing her wet tissues on the far side of the desk and the pile kept growing like an approaching iceberg.

"Sit down so we can discuss this."

"I don't want to," she said, and began sobbing

again.

"You can't have an affair with a board member!"

"I don't care!" she sobbed. "That bird is driving me crazy," she snapped, and ran to the window. "He's probably out there right now!" she insisted. Willy got up and hobbled to the window after her. "He must have heard me telling you about him 'cause he's gone." Willy looked out the window at the empty parking lot and saw the building's shadow in the late afternoon sun. The image of a large bird moved back and forth on the building's straight-lined edge just over him. Viola was right. If it was Coocochee, he had probably heard everything. Willy slammed the window shut and the large raven above him flew off.

"I'll tell him to stop following you," he said.

"I'll end it when I want to," she said. The door slammed and she was gone.

Her high-heeled clicks faded and it got quiet again. The only thing left of her being there was the pile of wet tissues to remind him of the generational chainsaw he had just walked into. His attempt at resolving the "high crimes and misdemeanors" within his tribe had failed miserably, and he hadn't the slightest idea what he was going to do next. What had become evident was that somehow the younger generation around him seemed to think that getting fired for bad typing was worse than having an affair with an older married man who was a board member. Today had replaced yesterday, but there wasn't a tomorrow in sight. Gratification seemed to be all that mattered to them and a lot more of his people had drifted backwards since Red Cloud, Crazy Horse, and Cochise were in charge. The fact was that no one seemed to be in charge anymore, and hadn't been for a long time.

It was a challenge...unexpected.

# Ted Jonathan

## *Thrift Shopper*

At Goodwill Thrift Shop
on Bronx Park East,
I hope to lighten some.

Hunting,
I might find anything,
from a saltshaker
to a wah-wah pedal …

But today I need –
to feel more alive.

& am intent on talking to Rosa,
the buoyant cashier.

In a cold hand
I grip my cover
a dollar paperback

& detour past some joker holding
court sporting a thick, writhing
gold-specked snake coiling
his neck & approach her:

Alone,
She's humming
along to the radio –

Our dark eyes meet.

"Hi," I say.

"Hi," she says.

I say, "I might get a snake."

Her small sweet face scrunches sour –
"I don't like it!"

I say, "Howwa boudda Chihuahua?"

"I will allow one Chee-hua-huá!"

Dreaming our whole life together,
I smile and say, "Thanks, Rosa."


## *Why I Wish I Were More Like Tony G.*


I know how much he loves live music,
but am in awe, that following a grueling
morning of dialysis, and an afternoon
on the job, he comes into view, one foot
slowly after the other, drawing nearer,
meeting me tonight at B.B. King's.

Seated across from one another,
at a small table, I'm most pleased to see
that his face has regained its color,
and that he can enjoy a scoop
of vanilla ice cream. Having no interest
in the featured act, a rocking singer/guitarist
named, Jackie Green, I'm here to spend
time with Tony, talk shit and share a laugh.
The man never complains.

Green, it turns out, is more than okay.
He sings, his fingers are nimble,
and his band's good too. It just doesn't
add up to much. After the show, Tony
would assess the performance aptly, saying,
"The sum is less than the parts."

But now the band's rocking, Tony's
eyes are shut, head's bopping. Happy
for him, on my feet, I tap into his groove,
for maybe thirty seconds, before owning
my lack of feel-good staying power …

As the set winds down, the audience
applauds, and Green says, "Thanks."
They exit the stage. And all's well –
but for an encore. They cover "Sugaree"
by the Grateful Dead, including
a long jam. But they're not the Dead,
and it's getting late.

When Tony leans over, to whisper
something into my ear, I'm glad to hear
him say, "This is fucking torture."
Knowing damn well that bad can
only get worse, I'm always ready to flee,
and say, "Let's get the fuck out of here."
"No," he says, "they might play something
I like next."

# Vincent J. Tomeo

## *101st Anniversary*

Here I sit on a park bench, one year later.
Something there is about the 100th anniversary.
It was celebrated with music,
Marine marching band, dignitaries, military officers,
a priest gave a benediction, too.

The National Anthem was played.
History recalled, remembered, honored, and respected.
A fallen hero was remembered with reverence.

One year later, the flag pole is stained, grape lemon
    ice,
smeared like a splatter on an ink blotter.
Bushes uncut, noise vibrates loudly, homeless men
    sleeping on benches.

Now, the people in this park don't even know his
    name!

A man is urinating behind a bocce court.
A woman is going through garbage.
Three men retrieving booze and drugs hidden in the
    bushes.

Today, June 7 is the 101st anniversary of Pvt. William
    Frederick Moore's death. He was killed in WW
    One, in the battle of Belleau Wood, France, June 7,
    1918, and no one is here.

# Brian James Lewis

## Wrenching On Dreams
### a garage poem

Wrenches turn silver and greasy chrome
in the half-darkness under an old Cadillac
up on jacks in the garage
The doctor in this place doesn't wear a gown
and this surgery isn't deathly quiet or super sterile
like the hospital uptown

Rock and Roll blasts and the Blues boogies from a
boom box covered with skulls and flames
Making those wrenches turn faster

Oil and grease runs like water-while ZZ Top sizzles
John Lee Hooker warns us that he's a madman – Yeah!
And Elmore James dusts his broom
Then disaster strikes when a clump of sharp rust flakes
land on the wrench turner's face making him curse
as they stick in eyes untouchable

By fingers smeared with dirt and grease. Don't blink!
Just slip, slide, and run for the house with its
orange smelling hand cleaner. Don't Blink!
Luckily, Q-tips wetted with saliva nab them
off the whiskery face with wild eyes
jammed up to the mirror, Ahhhh!
Back in the garage Chuck Berry is singing "Nadine"
This is the place where everything gets fixed and
      brought
back to life by wrenches that
Spin silver and greasy chrome in the semi-dark
The hot yellow work lights illuminate the scene like

it's a secret stage or carnival side show
The dog drinks water from his chrome bowl
and circles three times into his Mexican blanket
bed and sighs, drifting off into dreams
While the hands in the garage refuse to give up on
    theirs
Wrenches spin, oil and grease runs like water
The key is turned and the Cadillac belches
Loud black smoke into the cooling night air
clacking like a typewriter and coughing up a
lung "Hoook-a-lung-a! Hook-a-LUNG-A!
The engine screams and squeals while
the old car shudders like a cat in the bathtub
Dog jumps in the backseat and off they roar!
Into that deep blue night sky that is full of
ancient stars and dreams that might come true
When wrenches spin silver and greasy chrome

# Dana Stamps, II.

## Love Letters

I WROTE MY MISTRESS Cindy handwritten love letters, sent them to her P.O. box in Cincinnati so her husband wouldn't find out. She was a dusky-hued brunette with thick curly hair, and she would fly to California from Ohio to visit me every time she got the chance, which was often. But I hated to go to Ohio for any reason: too cold in the winter, too humid in the summer.

Several years into our affair, my letters, usually detailing what we would do at our next rendezvous, were missing from her dresser. By the time her warning reached me, I knew about the missing letters because her husband had tossed them, crumpled at my feet, pointing a gun at my face.

Darryl, a heavyset bald dumbass, yelled, spitting his words, *What do you have to say for yourself now, Mr. California?*

Indignant, I retorted that I didn't vow to be faithful to him before God and everyone at his wedding, and it was not me, but his wife who had betrayed him. He cried, and with his vision blurry, I snatched the revolver from his hand.

*Listen, Darryl, I did you a favor. Now you know you cannot trust Cindy; if you're going to shoot somebody, maybe it should be her?* I retorted. I let him go, kept the handgun as a souvenir.

Later, the crybaby cuckold divorced her, then she wanted to marry me! But how could I trust her when vows meant so little to her? She left me for a moneyed fool who would say *I do.*

# Morgan Smith

## Chaos on the Border

EARLIER THIS YEAR, I submitted an article about migrants – most of them from Honduras, Guatemala and El Salvador – who were being fed and housed in La Casa del Migrante, a migrant shelter in Juárez, Mexico, while awaiting their asylum hearings with US officials. Unlike the deplorable conditions in US facilities, such as the one in Clint, Texas, La Casa offers a level of care, security and respect that has to be seen to be believed. I've visited eight times now, often with my wife Sherry, and we always take much needed food and clothing.

This has marked a major addition to the work I do on the border. For most of the eight years during which I have been making trips at least once a month, my focus was on the people who live along the border, documenting their struggles in an environment of violence, poverty, and a lack of government support. These are not people who have an interest in migrating

to the US. Besides, the number of migrants had been going down dramatically; in addition, it seemed that President Trump's focus on the wall was off target since most of those who are in the US illegally came here legally and just overstayed their visas.

That changed with this dramatic surge of migrants. Not only have the numbers been staggering, but the majority are now families rather than young men, making their care much more complicated. In addition, the level of political hostility between Republicans and Democrats has reached a new level of intensity, making it even more unlikely that rational solutions can be reached.

Nonetheless, my involvement in the migrant issue has led to three thoughts.

**The Wall.**

This is clearly a red flag issue for Democrats but I would ask my party to consider the following. The photo that leads off my earlier article was taken from the Mexico side of the wall as it stretches towards El Paso,

Texas. It looks like it goes on forever. On the Friday before this Easter, however, my wife Sherry and I followed a narrow dirt road along the US side of this wall in search of the spot where migrants were coming through. We quickly discovered that the wall simply ends as you near the rugged Monte Cristo Rey. This astonished us. Why build a massive and very expensive wall and then just have it end so that anyone could walk across?

Nearby we found the militia camp. They were in fact acting as lookouts for the Customs and Border Patrol (CBP).

A month later, I drove to the same spot just as a dozen young migrants came running across.

Initially I was opposed to more wall construction but now it seems obvious that *we should have a complete wall in places like the El Paso/Juárez area where several million people are congregated.* (Author's emphasis)

I'm in favor of expanding immigration. We currently give some form of resident status to about one million migrants a year and I would expand that. But that has to be our decision. As Americans, we have to be the ones to decide who can enter our country. *To quote Thomas Friedman in a recent column, 'without a high wall, too many Americans will lack confidence that we can control our borders, and they therefore will oppose the steady immigration we need.'* (Author's emphasis) If we have to expand some border walls to get better control, we should do so.

**Humanity versus Dollars.**

When we Americans provide services to the needy, we measure our commitment by dollars. So many dollars for the mentally ill or for school teachers or for meals for kids. On the Mexican border, however, the money isn't available and government support doesn't exist. The services that are available are provided by private organizations and/or individuals. What characterizes their success is caring and humanity.

This also applies to the way migrants have been treated in the US. The terrible conditions at Clint, Texas are characterized by a lack of caring, not a lack of money.

In contrast, take a look at Deming, New Mexico (pop. 14,000). In mid May, the CBP suddenly dumped several hundred migrants in Deming and told town officials that it was their problem. The response from the townspeople as well as volunteers from all over New Mexico has been astounding. Just as  on the Mexican border, the humanity of individuals is often more important than mere dollars. That is the bright side of this otherwise heart breaking situation.

**The Remain in Mexico program.**

When people from other countries come to our border and ask for asylum, they are exercising a right. They are not doing anything illegal. Historically, they have had an initial screening with the CBP and then allowed to enter the US and stay with other family members pending their final judicial hearing. The recently announced Remain in Mexico program is a dramatic change and a *very dangerous one* that will require those applicants to return to Mexico to await this judicial hearing. Already, well over 10,000 migrants have been returned just to the Juárez area. What does this mean?

In the first six months of 2019, there were 775 murders in Juárez. Compare this to 250 in Chicago and 135 in New York, two cities that are dramatically larger than Juárez with its population of about 1.5 million. Is it humane to force these migrants – most of them from other countries with few resources and no contacts in Juárez

itself – back into such a dangerous environment? Shelters like La Casa del Migrante can't come close to handling them all, so they will be dispersed and essentially moved out of sight. Unlike the Clint, Texas situation, there will be no way that the press or concerned members of Congress can advocate for them.

Tomorrow, I'm heading to Juárez again, the car already packed with food and clothing. My wife, Sherry is going to pass this time; the extreme heat gets to her as well as my marathon pace. Once you start something like this, however, you can't just quit. That's what I have learned from the people I have come to know on the border. At some point you just become a part of them and you have to keep going.

Photos:

Pages 93 and 95: Migrants running for the border
Page 94: The end of the border wall to the west of El

Paso and Juárez.
Page 96: Kids looking through the border wall. They are on the Mexican side.
Page 97: Padre Javier Calvillo, the director of La Casa del Migrante and the key person in terms of migrant care in Juárez. He is with Sister Betty Campbell, a nun who has run programs for women in Juárez for the last 23 years.

# John N. Miller

## *The Swan Song Of J. Nelson Prufreed*

I grow old . . . I grow old . . .
I shall wear my long johns when fall days turn cold.
Too old for yet another late-May scorcher,
I sit out on our shaded porch
trying to catch a breeze. Our flower plot
has gone to weed. Blame it on my torpor,
lassitude, some say, or lethargy,
or too much pessimism.
                                    Sick
of our deranged two-party politics,
too weak to be an Independent,
I'm now a Neo-Hypochondriac,
measuring out my life with costly pills,
avoiding sunstroke and rheumatic chills,
and papering the seats in public johns
before I lower my bare buttocks on them.

But that's no singing lesson for my soul
as Yeats would have for ageing, scarecrow men.
As a young boy I was schooled
in the piano; soon enough I'll be
an organ donor. How do I get ready?
Should I press iron? Sweat, or play it cool?
I'll ply my senile sidestroke in a lukewarm swimming
        pool.

Then comes the torpor, mind and muscle slowed
almost to standstill, letting the weeds grow
dominant in my view of outdoors.

Torpor, lassitude, and lethargy –

my three-as-one, an old coot's trinity,
nothing to worship or write hymns about;
instead, I'd like a cygnet threnody.

Not knowing how swans vocalize their dying,
I'll grace a bullfrog's love song when I croak.


## *At a Fraternity Reunion*


Wives of aging celebrants –
matrons plumped together, sidelined
like potential chaperones – smile indulgence
for the juvenile nicknames and backslapping
rituals of Brotherhood.

"Boys will be boys." They know
their publicly respected men –
the sulks and sudden tantrums,
prodigality, unbroken habits,
need for mothering.

Now it's good ol' boy time –
high jinx, low x-rated jokes
boozy but not so drunken
as to call for them to interfere.
Then they see that they'll be serenaded

and hear at first what they expect –
wavering, slightly off-key
pledges of undying loyalty
to three Greek letters
and to themselves, old-time fraternity

sweethearts, now

matriarchs of their suburban culture;
then the singing rises, strident,
loud, aggressive, militant,
belted out in lockstep unison.

Are they wives of lovable old boys?
of blood-sworn brothers?
of combative veterans?
Wives of hardened celebrants
huddle together, frowning.

# Sheryl L. Nelms

## South Dakota Badlands

some compare it to Dante's Hell

but it is better

spend the night
in a Coleman tent
feel the land

watch thunderheads
boil themselves up
into monster mushrooms
that variegate to pink
cotton candy
at sunset

then in the dark

look up
to the constellations
see the Big Dipper
so much closer

and magnified

feel the pureness
of prairie rain
on buffalo
grass

smell the damp dirt

listen to the gentle
grumble in the west
building to a roaring rumble

followed by phosphorescent
stripes of white
light

and imagine
tyrannosaurus rex

clomping
here

# Bernard Haske

## *As Emma Upstairs Plays The Piano for Fritz Gollery*

Don't quote me the pertinent passages –
remind me of Peter and Thomas –
their denials – redemption –
remind me of women's love –
Mary – their love –
       woman on the Giant parking lot 8 a.m. –
*I need help* she says to anyone who could hear her –
I heard her – gave her nothing – used her – for this.

# Ben Terry

## Hope vs. Quality of Life

"BEN, YOU TORE A LIFE from the fabric of the universe." Is how a friend recently put it. He is right. That's exactly what I did on July 4th, 2005, when I shot a man named, Benny Lee Ladd, in the chest with a 12 gauge shotgun. That's been almost fourteen years ago, as of the time of this writing. It was just last week that my friend, Mike, uttered those words to me. Never before had I heard the moment framed so succinctly.

My lawyer said it was no different than a soldier at war. The immediate difference most obvious to me was that simile leaves out the part we were both drug addicts living poorly chosen lives. The jury did not agree with my lawyer either. Regardless of the particulars one way or the other, two things are unequivocally true: I ripped the thread of a life from the fabric of the universe, and because of that, a jury found me guilty of murder in the first degree, sentencing me to life without the possibility of parole.

I was 24 by the time of my hearing. My daughter, who was seven, had the wherewithal to ask if I would be home for her high school graduation. An event eleven years away, which would have been a life and a half to her at that point. (I later learned he too had children.)

His family's anguish and vitriol was palpable. As his mother sat on the stand and read her prepared statement at my sentencing, I might have been the only one who did not gasp, when she espoused her heartfelt desire that I be abused nightly for the rest of my life. In that moment, I was measuring the world through the eyes of a parent as I weighed her words in my mind. It's a shame, I hadn't actually started thinking like a parent sooner. Then perhaps the ugliness I'd helped create would in fact not exist.

I'm 37 years old now, and my daughter is 20 with two daughters of her own. My son is 17, and that's all I really know about him now which is also an ugly truth. There are a lot of ugly things about life and humanity.

The state weighed my life and choices and deemed me a danger to society. This was not the legacy I had in mind, and so I've spent the last thirteen years striving to prove them wrong. And I'm not done, but I recognize there could very well come a day when my hope will be outweighed by an irreparably diminished quality of life – be it sickness and disease, I become too weak to defend myself in here, or I lose the loved ones I have left – so I wrote a piece of legislation that pits "reason to hope" against the innate "ability to hope."

I call it the "Killing Time" Bill. It seeks to put the legal right to die in the hands of inmates serving the sentence of life without the possibility of parole (LWOP) here in Missouri – a sentence currently being served by approximately 1,500* inmates in the state.

This is no simple kill order – or as some opponents might claim an "easy out." Points in the bill include: a minimum age requirement of 25* (based on scientific research of brain development and decision making skills in teens and young adults); good behavior requirements rivaling and exceeding that of current parole board standards; a mental evaluation and mandatory "End of Life Counseling"; a void clause involving a "civility contract", should the inmate decide to commit a drug offense or violent crime between the application process and the ELD (End of Life Date); a two-year adjustment period after the petition is granted; and a clause that would mandate the MDOC (Missouri Department of Corrections) to make payment to the Missouri Department of Education the annual yearly cost of incarceration for the projected remainder of what would have been the inmate's natural life.

An average cost of $1 million per inmate over the span of their lifetime means the KTB's education clause could equate to tens of millions of dollars in as little as a decade. Although it seems macabre to think in such terms as blood money, economics have become the backbone of support for mass incarceration. Not only taxpayers' dollars but billions in corporate gain are at stake within the prison industrial complex.

The KTB's education clause quarters no sense of martyrdom. It bears a twofold purpose and a powerful message. Not only does it provide a degree of final restitution, it allows taxpayers' dollars to net a greater return on a far greater investment, in that education has statistically proven the most successful deterrent to recidivism, and diversion mechanism to the flow of children entering the prison pipeline. (Single parent households with an absentee father also increase the likelihood of incarceration by close to fifty percent. Just this week I was told to look out for a boy coming into the prison. A boy whom I had watched grow up in the visiting room of a facility I'd spent the previous decade in.)

In truth, it's already up to me, just as it is for any free person. The fact is, I live around the corner from the Death Wish Factory. If I really wanted to die today, I wouldn't be asking the public legislature for permission. I just don't want to die in the same manner I was living before I came to prison, and I'm not the only one.

As human beings, we seek out happiness. Joy is our greatest desire. As proof, we run after all manner of things in pursuit of it. The answer to the question is the same for everyone. Purpose. Happiness doesn't come in the same package for everyone, but I do believe that every human being longs to feel valuable and needed, to know that all "this", the good, bad, and ugly, of life isn't for naught.

Recently, I had the honor of being told I am a good friend and an inspiration. The individual went on to express lament over their own late start at working toward being a better person. I had to stop them and explain. Behind the man they see me as today, is a dead human being, and a string of broken and wounded people. A lot of people have paid a very high price for me to be what I've become today. Not to say I merit being anybody's pinnacle, just that I know for certain what kind of man I never want to be again.

I remember being told the funeral procession for the young man I killed was barely five cars long. I don't know how true that is, but I do know that it wasn't because he lacked value as a human being. What I know of him, his life lacked vision, much the same as mine did at the time. Though already into our 20's, we were two broken youths, blindly warring against everything we thought might hurt us.

"Everything" didn't include the normal list of dangers life holds, like drugs, guns, and actual insurgency, just the truth. We were fighting against the way that we felt. That is, we wanted to stop feeling lost, weak, and helpless. If that doesn't make sense it's because, by definition, insanity never does. It becomes a fitting example of poor social adjustment – (that's the kind of phrase they use to determine the safest place to put you for the betterment of society) – two young men who couldn't quite figure out what "being a real man" actually looked like, and youthful, arrogant, selfish pride that wouldn't allow them to confess their ignorance.

Looking back, I realize that several people lying in my wake saw me coming and chose to sacrifice themselves, their money, their time, and their hearts to save me, even when it seemed in vain; because they dared to hope.

Of the men polled on their support of the *Killing*

*Time Bill*, 70% say they would like to have the legal option to tap out in the event life finally becomes untenable. Nearly half of those men admitted to having already planned an exit strategy for the day hope was no longer an option for them.

Here is what I meant when I said I live next to the Death Wish Factory: any one of us, on the weight of a few whispered words, in two days' time could be in possession of a needle and enough drugs to never wake up again. But the only purpose in that death would be self-serving and meaningless. Chancing the cardinal rule against redundancy in writing, I'm saying 24 of the 32 men, society, by her policies has judged incorrigible and irredeemable, would prefer to honor the law, even in death.

This is a sentiment that should not be confused with the recent laws passed in Europe that allow the terminally ill and those suffering from diseases, such as cancer, schizophrenia and severe clinical depression, the right to clinically assisted death. (Interestingly, the European Court Of Human Rights [July 9th, 2013], has ruled life without parole inhumane.)

The potential political and social implications of the *Killing Time Bill* loom heavy. Aspects of the KTB bring to mind Kevorkianesque questions of morality and ethics. While the death penalty issue is arguably as polarizing as abortion, it holds less debatable ambiguity surrounding the question of what constitutes a life. Unlike abortion, however, personhood is secondary to the question of distributable and dismissible rights. *To date, more states have outright banned the death penalty, deeming it unethical, than have banned abortion.

Human rights groups have long since labeled life without parole "The Other Death Penalty" on the grounds it is simply a slower and more torturous version of its relatively expedient counterpart. (An argument they raise under the umbrella of the 8th and 14th

Amendments, and federal court rulings on deliberate indifference.) But even among that camp, feelings toward the actual death penalty are sometimes divided. Among the debates against use of the death penalty, the ethics of making such a final judgment in a legal system fraught with human error – both omissive and permissive – have been a major point of contention.

Despite so great a margin for error, among those states who still utilize the death penalty with relative gusto, local courts and even governors seem wary of weighing in on the matter once the trial has concluded – often times in the face of mitigating evidence that should cast a doubtful shadow.

*Since Clinton's 1996 ADEPA act, soaring incarceration numbers, despite relatively stable crime rates across the nation over the last 30 years shed ample light on the lark of "Tough on Crime" policies favored at election time. Many politicians are making the slow turn with the chic watch phrase "Smart on Crime," borrowed from prison reform advocates long in the battlefield ranging from economists and criminal justice majors to social welfare constituents.

**The problem?** When it comes time to enact meaningful legislative, administrative, and judicial change, the most invasive and promising solutions appear to require political suicide, and will likely necessitate a guiding hand for years to come. Although the public has become largely quick to rally around the call to "Get Smart on Crime," as "Getting Tough on Crime" is proving too mindless, too expensive, and too tough a solution, public resistance and fear of truncated political careers arise when the smartest solutions, to date, have been presented.

**Fear mongering and feeding hostility** are unfortunately ever present political tactics well known for their ability to trump reason. Ideas, like dropping minimum mandatory sentencing and shifting the focus of incarceration to formal education co-opted with cognitive behavioral modification as the pillar of rehabilitation, meaning translatable preparation for social reintegration and legitimate career paths, can get people easily riled when they themselves might be struggling with the cost of college tuition, and/or have been personally impacted by crime. Here the conversation becomes further muddled.

**Privilege vs. Right** *vis-à-vis* Education vs. Public Safety. At the point of incarceration, the argument moves beyond Republican or Democratic patter and finger pointing over opportunity sans ideal social systems. The nation's future and public safety should naturally become the sole focus.

Much like a parent realizing the discipline they choose for their child does not come without consequence to themselves, society must recognize the chain of criminal punishment has two ends, and one of them is indelibly attached to the public. Enters the question, what is our most logical solution to the problem of public safety regarding our failed crime and punishment policies?

*Over 95% of those incarcerated will be returning to the streets. *Current statistics show 80% will likely recidivate within the first five years. *Violent crimes, such as murder, coincidentally show a significantly lower re-offense rate than any other crime. However, the reduced likelihood of recidivism planes off dramatically beyond the 20-year mark of incarceration. *Missouri's prison system has grown to over 30,000. That is nearly a 100% increase in less than 20 years. At a cost of approximately $21,500 per inmate, this accounts for $645,000,000 of MDOC's $700+ million dollar budget. *This figure does not include the multimillion dollar contract for DOC's medical care provider, Coruzon.

The collective message echoed down through history has been "Crime doesn't pay". *Considering the quip by economist Milton Friedman "There's no such thing as a free lunch," we can no longer afford to ignore our chosen approach has proven more than we can chew.

**Five years after the Supreme Court ruled** juvenile life without sentences to be unconstitutional, Missouri has openly continued to circumvent the decision, further tying up an already congested and overburdened judicial system because the onus of meaningful reform appears to be too great in the current climate and foreseeable future.

Supporters of the *Killing Time Bill* say they hope to give law makers the "easy out," and the rest of the public some carefully considered insight, to perhaps overall lessen the moral and ethical burden of deciding what constitutes justice.

**What to do?** As one pundit speaking on the incarceration issue in Texas said, we've taken a lot of people and locked them up for a very long time. And it's a plan that simply does not work. So we need to take a hard look and figure out which ones we are actually scared of, and which ones we are just mad at, and figure out how to let them go. A sentiment that Missouri has thus far shown unwilling to consider.

**IF NOT/THEN...** The *KTB* provides inmates an avenue to petition the sentencing court under "Option A" for a "meaningful and realistic opportunity for release" based on a comprehensive list of rehabilitative requirements. If denied, the petitioner then has the opportunity to request "Option B" – an application for an ELD (End of Life Date) granted upon meeting the same comprehensive list of rehabilitative requirements. Hope vs. Quality of Life.

Human beings are either capable of change or they are not. And if not, then what is the humane and responsible thing to do?

The *Killing Bill State/* see more on Facebook.

*In the face of information restriction due to my incarceration, I was not able to verify as updated the assertions marked by asterisks.

# Trajectory

## Author Profiles

**Marion Byers**, who holds a Masters in both English and Social Work, is a retired University of Kentucky professor. She also worked in the cable and TV marketplace and as a researcher for *The Blood-Horse* magazine. Marion has a son, a daughter, and four grandchildren. She lives and writes in Lexington with her husband of fifty years.

**R.T. Castleberry** is an internationally published poet and critic. He was a co-founder of the Flying Dutchman Writers Troupe and co-editor/publisher of the poetry magazine, *Curbside Review*. His work has appeared in *The Alembic, Santa Fe Literary Review, Adelaide Literary Magazine, Roanoke Review, Misfit* and *Trajectory*. He lives and writes in Houston, Texas.

**Blair Ewing** has published poems in recent issues of *Gargoyle* and *Grasslimb* and his translations of Catullus have appeared in *Acumen* [UK], *Lilliput Review, Poetry Salzburg Review* and *Poetry Ireland Review*. He lives north of Baltimore, which he still considers "up South."

**Rod Farmer** has had over a thousand poems, essays, book reviews and scholarly articles published, including three poetry chapbooks. He is professor emeritus at the University of Maine at Farmington.

**Bernadine Fillmore** has been writing poetry for nearly 40 years. She is a published writer, and has read and performed her poetry on many occasions in many venues in the Greater Newark, New Jersey area. She was a volunteer for 15 years at the Trinity Church Food Pantry on Hawkins St. in Ironbound. She has been active in collecting free fun and educational resources for children for many years. She is an active citizen who takes part in decisions in Newark city life. She has received a number of awards, among them A "Neighborhood Heroes" Award from Ironbound Community Corporation in 2004 for her Community Service at the Food Pantry, an award from Newark Emergency Services for Families for serving on their Homeless Advisory Board, and most recently a Certificate of Appreciation for Leadership and Support from New Community Corporation on May 22, 2012.

**Steve Flairty** is a teacher, public speaker and an author of six books: a biography of Kentucky Afield host Tim Farmer and five in the *Kentucky's Everyday Heroes* series, including a kids' version. Steve's "Kentucky's Everyday Heroes #4," was released in 2015. Steve is a senior correspondent for *Kentucky Monthly*, a weekly *KyForward* and *NKyTribune* columnist and a former member of the Kentucky Humanities Council Speakers Bureau.

At age 27 **David Goldstein** was appointed Michigan's Deputy Appellate Defender. He learned some of the kindest people did awful things. Circumstances can fell anyone. He learned the criminal justice system judges acts instead of people. There are "primitive" African tribes with better justice systems. After six years reversing more than 60 felony convictions, David decided to pursue other interests. He now has more than 70 short stories published in 10 countries, as well as 5 poems. He has recently been nominated for a WW Norton Best Creative Nonfiction Award.

**Eric Greinke's** poems and essays have been published in a wide range of international literary magazines since the late sixties, most recently in *Rosebud, The North Dakota Quarterly, The Taj Mahal Review* and *The Schuylkill Valley Journal*. This is his second appearance in *Trajectory*. His most recent books are *Shorelines* (Adastra Press, 2018) and *Invisible Wings* (Presa Press, 2019). Contact him at www.ericgreinke.com.

**Bernard Haske** is retired from *The Baltimore Sun* and lives near Baltimore. His first book of poems, *The Color of Humans*, not quite an international bestseller, is available on Amazon. He is seeking a publisher for his second collection.

**Mark Havlik's** work has appeared in *Trajectory, The Hungry Chimera, Anomaly (FKA Drunken Boat )*, the anthology *Flying South, Kaleidoscope, Chaleur Magazine, Passing Through, South Florida Arts Journal, Santa Fe Writers Project Literary Journal,* and *Washington The Magazine.*

**Chris Helvey's** short stories have been published by numerous reviews and journals, including *Kudzu, The Chaffin Journal, Best New Writing, New Southerner, Modern Mountain Magazine, Bayou, Dos Passos Review,* and *Coal City Review.* He is the author of *Yard Man* (Wings ePress), *One More Round* (short story collection – Trajectory Press), *Snapshot* (novel – Livingston Press), *Whose Name I Did Not Know* (novel – Hopewell Publications), and *Claw Hammer* (short story collection – Hopewell Publications). Helvey currently serves as Editor in Chief of *Trajectory Journal.*

**Anthony Herles** has taught English at both the high school level and college level. His poems and short stories have appeared in various literary magazines such as *Chronogram, The Lyric, Barbaric Yawp,* and *Trajectory.*

**Stephanie Hiteshew** lives in Columbia and Baltimore, Maryland depending on the day. She enjoys reading foreign poets and staying in contact with poets across the country. Stephanie has been previously published by *Propaganda Press, Barbaric Yawp, Bear Creek Haiku,* and others.

**J.S. Kierland** is a graduate of the University of Connecticut, and did postgrad at Hunter College where he won the New York City playwright's award. He was given a full scholarship to the Yale Drama School and after receiving his MFA became playwright-in-residence at Lincoln Center, Brandeis University, and the Lab Theatre. In Hollywood, he wrote two films, was resident playwright at the LAAT, where he founded the successful LA Playwright's Group, and went on to join Camelot Artists. He has published a novella, edited two books of one-act plays, written four films, and has over eighty publications of his short stories in literary collections, reviews and magazines around the U.S., including, *Playboy, Fiction International, Trajectory,* and many others. Underground Voices published his book *15 Short Stories* in 2014 and his 2015 novella titled, *Hard To Learn.*

Born and raised in the Bronx, **Ted Jonathan** currently lives in New Jersey. His latest poetry collection *Run* was published by NYQ Books (2016). He is very pleased to again have poetry published in *Trajectory.* He can be contacted at: theodorejon@yahoo.com

**John P. (Jack) Kristofco** has published over 700 poems and 60 short stories in about 200 different publications, including: *Folio, Rattle, Bryant Literary Review, Cimarron Review, Fourth River, Stand, The MacGuffin, Sierra Nevada Review, Blueline, Slant, Snowy Egret, and The Storyteller.* He has published three collections of poetry (most recently *The*

*Timekeeper's Garden* from The Orchard Street Press, at www.orchpress.com) and is currently putting together a book of short stories.

**Brian James Lewis** is a disabled poet, writer, and book reviewer, for whom writing is as important as breathing. After an accident left him with spinal injuries and mental health problems, Brian turned to writing as a second life. His work has appeared in the *Lowestoft Chronicle, Trajectory, The Hickory Stump, SLAB, Econoclash Review, Hellnotes* and *Damaged Skull Writer.* When time allows, Brian repairs vintage typewriters and uses them for first drafts. You can keep up with him on Twitter @skullsnflames76 or at: http://damagedskullwriterandreviewer.com

**Jack Phillips Lowe** is a proud Chicago-area resident. His poems have appeared in *Barbaric Yawp* and *Two Drops of Ink*, among other outlets. His most recent book is *Flashbulb Danger: Selected Poems 1988-2018* (Middle Island Press, 2018). Lowe currently hangs his hat in Addison, Illinois, an enchanted kingdom of foreclosed houses and fast food restaurants.

Though born in Ohio (1933), **John N. Miller** grew up in Hawai'i (1937-1951). He retired in 1997 from teaching literature and writing at his undergraduate alma mater, Denison University, and now lives with his wife Ilse in a retirement community in Lexington, VA.

**Sheryl L. Nelms** is from the Flint Hills of Kansas. She graduated from South Dakota State University. She's had over 5,000 articles, stories and poems published, including twenty individual collections of her poems. She's the fiction/nonfiction editor of *The Pen Woman Magazine*, the National League of American Pen Women publication and a four-time Pushcart Prize nominee. Extensive credits listing @ Sheryl L. Nelms at www.pw.org/directory/featured

**Beth Paulson** lives in Ouray County, Colorado where she leads the Poetica Workshop and co-directs the Open Bard Literary Series. She taught English at California State University Los Angeles for 22 years. Her poems have been widely published in national journals and anthologies and have four times been nominated for Pushcart Prizes. Beth's fifth book, *Immensity*, was published in 2016 by Kelsay Books. In May 2019 Beth was appointed the first Poet Laureate of Ouray County.

**Cathy Porter's** poetry has appeared in *Plainsongs, Homestead Review, California Quarterly, Hubbub, Cottonwood, Comstock Review,* and various other journals. She has two chapbooks available from Finishing Line Press: *A Life In The Day* (2012), and *Dust And Angels* (2014), as well as two chapbooks published by Dancing Girl Press in Chicago: *Exit Songs* (2016), and *16 Days* (2019). Cathy is a two-time Pushcart Prize nominee, and serves as a special editor for the journal *Fine Lines* in Omaha, NE, where she lives with her husband Lenny and their dog Marley, and cats Cody and Mini.

**Alden Reimonenq** was born and raised with deep roots in New Orleans, Louisiana. Windstorm Creative published his collection of poetry, *Hoodoo Headrag*, in 2001. He has also published poetry, fiction, reviews, and essays in *MELUS, The James White Review, African American Review, Alura, Poet, Berkeley Poetry Review, In the Family, Kuumba, Frontiers: San Francisco's News Magazine, Maryland Review, The Journal of Homosexuality, Trajectory,* and the collections: *Gents, BadBoys and Barbarians: New Gay Male Poetry, Milking Black Bull: Eleven Gay Black Poets,* and *When Love Lasts Forever: Male Couples*

*Celebrate Commitment*. Living in Palm Springs, CA, Reimonenq has completed his first novel.

**Robert Ronnow's** most recent poetry collections are *New & Selected Poems: 1975-2005* (Barnwood Press, 2007) and *Communicating the Bird* (Broken Publications, 2012). Visit www.ronnowpoetry.com.

**George J. Searles** teaches English and Latin at Mohawk Valley Community College and has also taught creative writing on Pratt Institute's upstate campus and graduate courses for New School University. In addition to many poems in literary journals, he has published three volumes of literary criticism and eight editions of a widely-used writing textbook. He is a former Carnegie Foundation New York State "Professor of the Year."

**Morgan Smith** is a former member of the Colorado House of Representatives and Colorado Commissioner of Agriculture. He can be reached at Morgan-smith@comcast.net.

**Matthew J. Spireng's** book *What Focus Is* was published by WordTech Communications. His book *Out of Body* won the 2004 Bluestem Poetry Award and was published by Bluestem Press. He won The MacGuffin's 23rd Annual Poet Hunt in 2018, judged by Alberto Rios, and is an eight-time Pushcart Prize nominee. He is also the author of five chapbooks.

**Dana Stamps, II.** has a bachelor's degree in psychology from Cal State University of San Bernardino, and has worked as a fast food server, a postal clerk, a security guard, and a group home worker with troubled boys. Poetry chapbooks *For Those Who Will Burn* and *Drape This Chapbook in Blue* were published by Partisan Press, and *Sandbox Blues* by

Evening Street Press. His short stories have appeared in *Chiron Review, Left Behind*, and *Trajectory*.

**t. kilgore splake** ("cliffs dancer") lives in a tamarack location old mining row house in the ghost copper mining village of calumet in michigan's upper peninsula. as an artist, splake has become a legend in the small press literary circles for his writing and photography. his most recent book is *ghost light* published by gage press in battle creek, michigan. splake is currently working on a new collection of poems that has the title *sunflower wisdom*.

**Ben Terry** is a poet and writer in residence at JCCC (a level 5 prison) in Jefferson City, MO where he is serving life without parole. His works have also appeared in *Colore, J Journal* and *Hanging Loose*. Two things Ben says the world should forever be cognizant of: a ramen soup's versatility has the power to amaze; and if you know a child unaware of their self-worth, living a life without purpose and direction, you are failing them.

**D.L. Tickel** is a songwriter, poet, fiction writer, and a student of literature, German and French Existentialism, and aspects of life that so often go unnoticed. His work has been published by *Ginger Hill* and *Trajectory*.

**Vincent J. Tomeo** is a poet, archivist, historian and community activist. For 36 years a New York City public high school teacher, teacher of American history. Presently volunteering at the 9/11 Tribute Center Museum at ground zero. Vincent is published in the *New York Times, Comstock Review, Mid-America Poetry Review, Edgz, Spires, Tiger's Eye, Byline, Mudfish, The Blind Man's Rainbow, The Neo Victorian/Cochlea, The Latin Staff Review,* and *Grandmother Earth (VII thru XI), etc.* To date, he has 878 published poems/essays; is winner of 105 awards; and done 127 public readings.

**Parker Towle** retired after fifty years of practicing and teaching neurology. He began writing poems in 1966 and has placed 260 poems in magazines and published 7 books of poems. He lives with his wife of 64 years in northern New Hampshire where after a 5-minute drive they can stand straight, reach out and touch four to five thousand foot mountains.

**Tamra Wilson's** work has appeared in *Epiphany, storySouth, The New Guard* and elsewhere. She is the author of *Dining with Robert Redford & Other Stories* and co-editor of *Idol Talk: Women Writers on the Teenage Infatuations That Changed Their Lives* (McFarland, 2018). She writes a slice-of-life column in North Carolina, and is a Road Scholar presenter for the NC Humanities Council.

**ONE MORE ROUND** contains stories by Chris Helvey published between 1977 and 2015. Collected together for the first time anywhere, these 19 stories reveal the revolving artistic journey of one of America's unique writers.

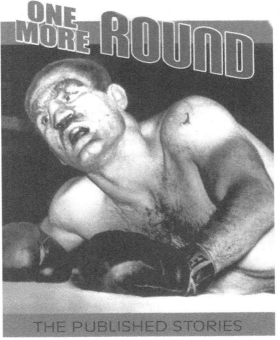

Chris Helvey

Available from Amazon

Paperback $10.00        E-book $3.00

**The Bluegrass Writers Coalition**
is a gathering of authors who work to promote literature in all forms across Kentucky. BWC members are active writers in all genres who believe that the printed word enhances the lives of writers and readers. The coalition endeavors to showcase writers and their works through discussions, readings, and book-signing events.

The BWC is open to all writers and usually meets the second Thursday of each month at 5:30 P.M. at Panera Bread, 101 Westbridge Drive in Frankfort. All writers are welcome to join. For more information, call Chris Helvey at 502-330-4746 or Michael Embry at 502-545-3367.

CPSIA information can be obtained
at www.ICGtesting.com
Printed in the USA
FSHW021006200320

9 781733 793629